What Every
Principal
Needs to Know About
Special
Education

Second Edition

What Every
Principal
Needs to Know About
Special
Education

Second Edition

Margaret J. McLaughlin

CORWIN PRESS
A SAGE Company

For information:

Corwin Press
A SAGE Company
2455 Teller Road
Thousand Oaks, California 91320
www.corwinpress.com

SAGE Ltd.
1 Oliver's Yard
55 City Road
London EC1Y 1SP
United Kingdom

SAGE Pvt. Ltd.
B 1/I 1 Mohan Cooperative
Industrial Area
Mathura Road, New Delhi 110 044
India

SAGE Asia-Pacific Pte. Ltd.
33 Pekin Street #02-01
Far East Square
Singapore 048763

Printed in the United States of America

Library of Congress Cataloging-in-Publication Data

McLaughlin, Margaret J.
What every principal needs to know about special education/Margaret J. McLaughlin. — 2nd ed.
      p. cm.
Includes bibliographical references and index.
ISBN 978-1-4129-6415-9 (cloth)
ISBN 978-1-4129-6416-6 (pbk.)

   1. Special education—United States—Administration. 2. Children with disabilities—Education—United States. 3. School principals—United States. I. Title.

LC4019.15.M178 2009
371.9—dc22   2008017825

This book is printed on acid-free paper.

          13   10   9   8   7   6   5

Acquisitions Editor:	David Chao
Associate Editor:	Desirée A. Bartlett
Production Editor:	Veronica Stapleton
Copy Editor:	Tina Hardy
Typesetter:	C&M Digitals (P) Ltd.
Proofreader:	Dennis W. Webb
Indexer:	Sheila Bodell
Cover Designer:	Lisa Riley

Contents

Preface to the Second Edition

Much has changed with special education since the first edition of *What Every Principal Needs to Know About Special Education* was published. At the time I finished the first book, the 2004 amendments of the Individuals with Disabilities Education Act (IDEA) had yet to be passed, and schools were in the early days of implementing the provisions within the No Child Left Behind (NCLB) legislation pertaining to students with disabilities. In the relatively few years since the publication of the first edition, a number of changes have occurred that I address in this book.

First, I recognize that school leaders everywhere have gained a lot of knowledge about special education over these past few years. The inclusion of students with disabilities as one of the subgroups that schools, school districts, and states are held accountable for under the Adequate Yearly Progress provisions of NCLB means that building administrators and other school leaders had to become aware of who these students are and what they are being taught. Furthermore, the NCLB regulations developed over the past several years provide even more guidance about how these students are to be assessed. This included defining two new subgroups of students with disabilities—those that may be held to alternate achievement standards and those students with disabilities who may be assessed against modified achievement standards.

These new rules have resulted in new procedures for developing Individualized Educational Plans (IEPs) and new assessments and reporting requirements. Principals will have to help general and special education teachers and the parents of students with IEPs understand the new procedures and the meaning of assessment results. However, the most important change and one that was just emerging at the time the first edition was published was the recognition that inclusion of students with disabilities in NCLB means far more than participating in state assessments. It is now very clear that every student with a disability is to receive instruction in the standard-driven curriculum that is the basis for instruction in general education classrooms. This is resulting in a movement to create "standards-based IEPs," which I also discuss in this book.

With the passage of the 2004 Individuals with Disabilities Education Improvement Act came other changes. (In this book, I continue to refer to the law as "IDEA" despite the name change). First, there was far greater alignment with NCLB. Congress sent a very clear message that special education was designed to improve student outcomes as indicated by the following quote from the law:

> *Having a disability in no way diminishes the right of individuals to participate or contribute to society. Improving educational results for children with disabilities is an essential element of our national policy of ensuring equality of opportunity, full participation, independent living, and economic self-sufficiency for individuals with disabilities.*

> Individuals with Disabilities Education
> Improvement Act of 2004, as amended

The law put even greater emphasis on students having access to general education curriculum, and the model presented in the first edition of this book that addressed special education as a support to a "curriculum continuum" has been updated to reflect new NCLB and IDEA policies.

The 2004 IDEA also made some changes to reduce the inappropriate identification of students with disabilities. These include "Response to Intervention" (RtI) and "Early Intervening Services" (EIS), and they are both discussed in this book. There is also a greater emphasis placed on prevention of behavior problems through requirements that "positive" behavioral supports and interventions be addressed in students' IEPs, which I discuss again in this edition.

Throughout the book, I include references and definitions to new policies as well as new resources for principals that pertain to important components of special education in the schools. For instance, I discuss new provisions for resolving disputes between parents and schools as well as new requirements for using "scientifically valid" or "evidence-based" practices.

In summary, I believe that the additions and revisions that have been made bring this book up to date with the most current policies as well as special education practice in today's schools.

Acknowledgments

I acknowledge the incredible organization and persistence of Valerie Foster in helping to prepare this manuscript.

I also appreciate the continued input and insights of Victor Nolet in thinking about this edition.

Corwin Press gratefully acknowledges the contributions of the following reviewers:

Jane Belmore, Adjunct Professor
Edgewood College
Madison, WI

Kim Benton, Executive Director
of Federal Programs and
Special Populations
Meridian Public Schools
Meridian, MS

Cathy Chamberlain, Assistant
Superintendent
Oswego City School District
Oswego, NY

John Enloe, Director of Pupil
Personnel Services
Sevier County Board of Education
Sevierville, TN

Kate A. Foley, Director of
Student Services
Lakewood City Schools
Lakewood, OH

Debi Gartland, Professor of
Special Education
Towson University
Towson, MD

Raymond Lowery, Principal
Alief Kerr High School
Houston, TX

About the Author

 **Margaret J. McLaughlin** is professor of special education in the Department of Special Education and associate director of the Institute for the Study of Exceptional Children and Youth at the University of Maryland, College Park.

She has been involved in special education all of her professional career, beginning as a teacher of students with emotional and behavior disorders and learning disabilities. She conducts research investigating educational reform and students with disabilities, including how students with disabilities are accessing standards and the impact of high stakes accountability on students with disabilities. She has consulted with numerous national, state, and local agencies and organizations on issues related to students with disabilities and the impact of standards-driven reform policies. She teaches graduate courses in disability policy and has written extensively in the area of school reform and students with disabilities.

Introduction

What Every Principal Needs to Know About Special Education

This book is intended for building administrators, those individuals who stand at the front line of educational reform and who are responsible for ensuring that every student has a fair and equal educational opportunity. The book may be different from others written for principals about special education. It does not focus solely on describing special education rules and procedures. Although the rules are important, this book goes further to help the principal understand both the intents of various policies as well as how to effectively implement them.

Principals have always been central to high quality special education programs in schools, but never more so than in today's climate of high standards and high stakes accountability. Today, school leaders need to have deep knowledge about special education and the students who receive these services. Until recently it was possible for a principal to delegate responsibility for special education to a special education teacher or department head. Now, principals must be involved with the education of any student because they are accountable for improving the achievement of all students.

The case of Mr. Baker illustrates this point.

Mr. Baker began his career as an elementary school principal in the mid-1990s and became a middle school principal several years ago. During his time as an administrator, Mr. Baker has witnessed a sea change in how students with disabilities are expected to be educated. When Mr. Baker first became a principal, he was under

(Continued)

(Continued)

great pressure from parents and the school district to "include" more of the students with IEPs into general education classrooms, particularly those students who were assigned to two special classes in his building. He found his special education budget strained by the need to hire more paraprofessionals who followed individual students with disabilities into classrooms. He also had to deal with teachers who did not want to include any of the students with IEPs in their classrooms, particularly those with more severe disabilities. However, Mr. Baker was very proud of the fact that he had very few complaints from parents and that the students with disabilities seemed to be accepted by other students in the building.

Then, in 2001, something changed. No longer was the quality of a special education program measured only by the time a student spent in general education or by how accepted students might feel. Suddenly, all students with disabilities were expected to meet annual achievement targets on the state assessment. The scores of these students were reported publicly, and the focus shifted to what students with disabilities were being taught and how well they were achieving. Initially, Mr. Baker was stunned. Surely, no one expected that all of the students with disabilities in his school would be tested on the same grade-level content. Moreover, the expectation was that these students would receive instruction in grade-level subject matter curriculum. After all, most of the students were two or more years below grade level in reading and math, and some were being taught functional living skills.

Mr. Baker soon found out that, indeed, all students were to be instructed in the same content. He did, however, learn that a small number of students could be held to alternate achievement standards.

Mr. Baker, like many of his colleagues, had entered a new era in public education, one in which he is now expected to be accountable for improving achievement of all students in his school. Mr. Baker was aware of how his low-income students had been progressing and how African American and Hispanic students were doing as a group, but he had never paid a great deal of attention to how his students with disabilities were doing. These responsibilities required that Mr. Baker and his staff gain new knowledge about special education, not just the new procedures about assessments and accountability but also how to ensure that all students in the school had a real opportunity to access the curriculum. Mr. Baker believed that his school was making progress. Scores for all students were generally on the upswing, although the scores of students with disabilities varied a lot across grades and years. Mr. Baker also believed that his teachers worked as a team. Then Mr. Baker was transferred to a new middle school where he continues to face the challenge of building a culture of achievement and high expectation for all students, and he faces more policy changes. These include the possibility of yet another type of assessment for students with disabilities based on "modified achievement standards" and new procedures for identifying learning disabilities. He also needs to be aware of how "transition planning" can help students with disabilities focus their high school careers and postsecondary goals. This book is intended to help Mr. Baker and his many colleagues in deepening their understanding of the many new special education policies as well as effective special education programs and strategies.

As more and more students with disabilities are educated in general education schools and classrooms, building principals have learned a great deal about who these students are and how they are educated, but there is still much to learn. The demands to improve the educational outcomes of these students are greater than ever. Special education policies and programs are changing and quickly demanding even greater knowledge on the part of school leaders. In this book, I provide an overview of the essential policies as well as effective practices for educating students with disabilities. I hope that the information in this book will help school leaders face the challenges of today's schools.

This book is organized into four sections: (a) Section I provides an overview of key current policies governing special education, (b) Section II discusses elements of quality special education programs and services, (c) Section III provides guidance on what is known about how to create effective special education, and (d) Section IV sums up what it means to be an effective leader in special education.

FIVE THINGS EVERY PRINCIPAL NEEDS TO KNOW ABOUT SPECIAL EDUCATION

Principals who are effective leaders of special education in their building should understand five key principles:

- Principals must understand the core special education legal foundations and entitlements. They should understand the intent or rationale of specific procedures. Simply following rules without understanding leads to cookie-cutter programs and pro forma compliance, not high quality special education.

- Principals need to understand that effective special education is truly individualized and matches instruction to the learning characteristics of students with disabilities.

- Principals must understand that special education is neither a place nor a program but a set of services and supports tailored to the needs of individual students so that they can progress in the general education curriculum.

- Principals must know how to meaningfully include all students with disabilities in standards, assessments, and accountability requirements.

- Principals need to know how to create the conditions within their schools that support effective special education practices and to finally integrate special education into all aspects of school improvement.

In Section I, I expand on these key ideas. I provide specific knowledge and practical strategies as well as examples for how to create effective special education. I hope that you find the book useful. I have spent many hours in schools and have been amazed by the knowledge and commitment of good principals. Good special education exists in schools with caring, strong, knowledgeable leaders. Principals can make a big difference in how students with disabilities and their families feel about school as well as what they learn. Because you are so important, I hope that you find the ideas and resources in this book valuable.

Creating Quality Special Education

Understanding the
Basics of Special Education

Key Ideas for Section I

➢ Students who receive special education are a very diverse group. A large number of these students share many characteristics with other low-achieving students.

➢ Special education is not a separate program or place—it is a system of supports and services in a school.

➢ Special education policies and practices can vary tremendously from state to state and district to district, but the core principles remain consistent.

The Individuals with Disabilities Education Improvement Act, or IDEA, is the federal law that governs special education. This law is a combination of both civil rights and education laws and has the following core requirements:

- All students with disabilities who are eligible to receive special education must be provided *a free, appropriate public education*, or FAPE. This means specially designed instruction and related services that meet the unique needs of an individual student and which should be provided in the *least restrictive* environment possible.

- The rights of every student with a disability and his or her family are ensured and protected through procedural safeguards.

WHAT IS AN APPROPRIATE EDUCATION?

The IDEA and the courts have defined an *appropriate* education as one that is provided in accordance with a child's Individualized Education Program (IEP) and is "reasonably calculated to confer benefit." The law assumes that a team of professionals, including a student's parents or guardian, is in the best position to determine what is appropriate for the student.

The IEP is central to special education. It is the official record of a child's legal entitlement to FAPE and defines the specially designed instructional services and supports and related services a student requires to meet his or her educational goals. The procedures and paperwork surrounding the IEP reflect the fact that this document represents a contract between the school district and the parent or guardian, so failure to follow procedures means that a student has been denied FAPE. There have been a number of changes made over the years to what must be included in an IEP as well as who must be involved in its development. The most recent changes were made to the IDEA in 2004.

There are three important areas to consider in developing an IEP: ensuring that including mandatory content is addressed, all required participants are included in decision making, and all notices and timelines are conducted according to procedures. Specific membership of an IEP team, as well as its content, procedures, and timelines, is determined by a combination of federal and state laws and local district procedures.

Beyond the mandatory procedures and content, what is "appropriate" for one student with a disability may not be appropriate for another. The core principle of FAPE is individualization.

> The IDEA defines related services to include such things as transportation, speech and language services, physical therapy, occupational therapy, technology, and recreation that an individual student may need to benefit from special education. There are certain restrictions on the type of medical services required, specifically those that require a physician.

> Two good sources for legal requirements are as follows:
>
> - Yell, M. (2006). *The law and special education* (2nd ed.). Upper Saddle River, NJ: Pearson Education, Inc.
> - Huefner, D. S. (2005). *Getting comfortable with special education law: A framework for working with children with disabilities.* Norwood, MA: Christopher-Gordon Publishers, Inc.

The current legal interpretation of "appropriate" comes from a U.S. Supreme Court decision, *Board of Education of the Hendrick Hudson School District v. Rowley* (1982), which determined that FAPE was not intended to mean that schools must maximize the potential of a student with a disability but must provide access to education that allows the student to "benefit" from educational programs and services. Other federal court cases have established that the educational benefit must be "more than trivial."

THE IEP

Since the IEP is central to special education, it is important for principals to understand the procedures for developing IEPs. (I discuss the IEP in more detail in Section II). There are a number of rules associated with developing an IEP, and it is essential that principals and teachers understand the procedures and timelines as developed by the local school district. However, the following provides a basic overview of the legal requirements associated with an IEP.

What Must Be in an IEP?

An IEP is a written document that must be developed for each student who is receiving special education or related services. The document has the following major components: assessment of the student's areas of need, individualized annual goals, measures of progress toward goals, services that will be provided, and the settings in which services will be provided.

Box 1.1   Each IEP Must Include, at Minimum, the Following Content

---

- A statement of the child's present levels of academic achievement and functional performance.
- A statement of measurable annual goals, including academic and functional goals designed to
  - Meet the child's needs that result from his or her disability to enable the child to be involved in and make progress in the general education curriculum.
  - Meet each of the child's other educational needs that result from the child's disability.

(Continued)

(Continued)

- For children with disabilities who take alternate assessments aligned to alternate achievement standards, a description of benchmarks or short-term objectives.
- A description of
  - How progress toward meeting the annual goals will be measured.
  - When periodic reports on the progress the child is making toward meeting the annual goals (such as through the use of quarterly or other periodic reports, concurrent with the issuance of report cards) will be provided.
- A statement of the special education and related services and supplementary aids and services, based on peer-reviewed research to the extent practicable, that will be provided to the child.
- A statement of any accommodations that are necessary to measure the academic achievement and functional performance of the child on state and district-wide assessments.
- If the IEP team determines that the child must take an alternate assessment instead of the regular state or districtwide assessment, there must be a statement of why the child cannot participate in the regular assessment and why the particular alternate assessment that will be used is appropriate for the child.

For students 16 years and older, or younger if determined appropriate by the IEP team, the IEP must include the following:

- Measurable postsecondary goals based on assessments related to training, education, employment, and, if appropriate, independent living skills.
- Transition services (including courses of study) needed to help the child in reaching those goals.

Who Develops the IEP?

The IEP team for each child with a disability includes the following:

- The parents of the student.
- Not less than one regular education teacher of the student if the student is, or may be, participating in the regular education environment.

- Not less than one special education teacher of the student or, where appropriate, not less than one special education provider of the student.
- A representative of the school district or public agency (who has certain specific knowledge and qualifications).
- An individual who can interpret the instructional implications (may also be one of the other members).
- At the discretion of the parent or the school district or other individuals who have knowledge or special expertise regarding the student, including related services personnel as appropriate.
- Whenever appropriate, the student with a disability. The student must be invited to attend if the purpose of the meeting will be to consider postsecondary goals and the transition services needed to reach those goals.

A member of the IEP team may not be required to attend the meeting if both the parent and district agree in writing. There are other team members who may not need to attend depending on the content of the IEP. However, principals should make themselves aware of the procedures established by their school district regarding team membership.

The IEP Meeting

Developing good IEPs can take time and requires good data and good communication. It requires that the IEP team have good assessment data and knowledge of the general curriculum as well as strategies and effective instructional practices that can meet diverse educational needs. Then, the team must have an opportunity to discuss and deliberate.

Schools may now conduct IEP meetings as well as other mandatory meetings involving parents or other providers using alternative means, such as video conferences and conference calls.

The IDEA requires that the team review a student's IEP periodically, but at least annually, to determine whether the annual goals are being achieved as well as to address the following:

- Any lack of expected progress toward the annual goals and in the general education curriculum.
- The results of any evaluations.
- Changes in a student's needs or other matters team members deem relevant.

If there is a need to change a student's IEP during the school year, there is no need to convene an IEP team meeting as long as the parent and district agree. Instead, a written amendment can be used to modify the student's current IEP.

The IEP and the Responsibility of the Principal

Beyond understanding the legal requirements for developing IEPs, there are several other areas where principal leadership is essential. For instance, principals can make sure that IEP teams have sufficient time to fulfill their responsibilities. Principals can support the IEP process logistically as well as being a proactive member of the IEP team. Principals also must ensure that IEPs are accessible to each regular education teacher, special education teacher, related services provider, and any other service provider who is responsible for implementing an IEP. Finally, principals must assume a leadership role in ensuring that services specified on an IEP are available and provided as prescribed. This may require negotiating for more resources outside the building.

> The following site has important training modules that can help in understanding and developing IEPs and other important requirements of IDEA: http://idea.ed.gov

THE LEAST RESTRICTIVE ENVIRONMENT

A second major entitlement in the IDEA is that a student with a disability be educated in the Least Restrictive Environment or LRE. This must also be an individual decision. The IDEA requires that students with disabilities be educated with their nondisabled peers to "the maximum extent appropriate." The regulations governing the IDEA also require that each district make available a continuum of placements as part of meeting the LRE requirement. These settings include regular classrooms, special classrooms, special schools, home instruction, and instruction in hospitals and institutions. The placements do not have to be used, but must be available should an IEP team determine that a specific student requires that setting.

The basic legal standard for determining the LRE requires that a student's IEP team first determine what constitutes an appropriate education for a student and then consider how to provide the special education and related services in the regular classroom within the school the student would have attended if he or she did not have an IEP. Removing a child from this setting can only occur when the nature or severity of the disability is such that education in regular class cannot occur even with the use of supplementary aids and services. A student cannot be educated outside of the regular classroom simply because of the nature of his or her disability or the types of services he or she may require.

Terms associated with LRE have included mainstreaming, reverse mainstreaming, integration, and inclusion. The first three terms often are interpreted to mean that special education is provided outside of the general classroom or school and that individual students move back into general education if they meet certain criteria. In contrast, inclusion begins with the assumption that every student is a member of a general education classroom and is expected to be educated within that classroom with his or her same-age peers. However, special education and related services may be provided in a variety of arrangements to support access to the general education curriculum.

Today, inclusion is the generally accepted goal for educating students with disabilities in regular schools and classrooms. However, in school districts all over the United States, we find students with disabilities being educated in separate settings. Across the United States, about half of all students with IEPs are educated in general education classrooms for 80% or more of the school day. But the percentages vary a great deal by disability. For example, on average, 55% of students identified as having a learning disability are educated 80% or more each day in general education classrooms compared to 35% of the students with emotional disturbance and 16% of students with mental retardation. As a group, Black students with IEPs are more likely to be educated in special education classes or schools. In 2005, nearly one fourth of Black students with disabilities and one fifth of Hispanic students were educated outside of the regular classroom more than 60% of the time compared to 13% of the White students. The disproportionate placement of minority students in special classes and settings is considered to be a major problem in special education and is now subjected to increased monitoring by states and the federal government.

Several federal court decisions have been instrumental in shaping decision making about LRE. Almost all of the cases have been brought by parents of students with moderate to significant disabilities. The decisions have resulted in a number of considerations for an IEP team that is deciding on a setting for a particular student.

Box 1.2   Basic Questions an IEP Team May Ask When Considering LRE

1. Can the special education and services offered in a segregated placement be feasibly provided in an inclusive setting?

2. Can education in the general education classroom be achieved if the right supplementary aids and services are provided?

(Continued)

(Continued)

3. If a student must be placed in a more restrictive setting, is the student integrated with nondisabled peers to the maximum extent possible?

4. Has the IEP team considered both the academic and nonacademic benefits of education and interaction with students without disabilities?

5. What is the effect of the student's presence on the teacher and other students, even with the appropriate supplementary supports and services?

6. What is the cost?

SOURCE: Yell (2006)

What Does the Research Tell Us About LRE?

LRE has been researched for over 40 years but most of the studies were conducted prior to 2000. The studies have looked at different students with characteristics and have measured effects on various outcomes. Hocutt (1996) reviewed a number of studies related to LRE and found that many were not of good quality. In general, the studies do not point to placement as *the* critical factor in student academic or social success. The classroom environment and the quality of instruction have more impact. The research does find slightly better academic outcomes for students with learning disabilities who receive special education in more specialized settings and higher dropout rates for students with emotional disturbance who are placed in general education classrooms without sufficient support. Students with mental retardation who are educated in general education classes have better social and communication outcomes and, overall, receive the most benefit from placement in supportive general education classrooms.

Research has also identified factors that influence whether inclusion is successful in a school. These include level of a school's commitment to inclusion, principal support and leadership, teacher attitudes, parent and family support, collaborative planning and teaching, focusing on both social and instructional inclusion, and peer acceptance and support. Finally, no studies have proven that including students with disabilities has a negative impact on students without disabilities.

Inclusion remains an important IDEA goal and recent changes to special education monitoring require states to set annual targets for increasing placements in regular schools and classrooms. The IDEA also requires that students with disabilities access the general education curriculum. This means that a student is not simply placed in a general education classroom but must receive meaningful opportunities to learn in the classroom. I discuss what it means to "access" the general education curriculum in Section II; however, the important fact for principals to remember is that LRE cannot be determined simply based on a student's disability category or because certain placements (e.g., resource room or special class) are or are not available. The LRE decision begins with determining for each student the appropriate special education and related services that allow the student access to the general education curriculum and then determining why those services cannot be provided within a regular class.

WHO IS ELIGIBLE FOR SPECIAL EDUCATION?

The current IDEA requirements for determining if a student is eligible to receive special education and related services are quite prescriptive. They evolved over time to address problems encountered in schools with failures to identify students with potential disabilities and delays in providing these students services as well as irresponsible and inappropriate placement of students in special education. The latter pertains mostly to students of different races, languages, and cultures whose achievement or behavioral problems were due to language or poor instruction and not disability.

Eligibility for special education is a two-prong decision. First, the student must be determined to have one of the 13 disabilities listed in the IDEA. States may use their own terms for these categories but they must assure the federal government that they are considering and evaluating students in all of the disability categories.

The second prong of the eligibility decision is to determine that disability creates an adverse effect on a student's learning. The IDEA is specific that a student's achievement problems cannot be due to poor instruction, language, or culture.

Some students with disabilities may require accommodations to access general education curriculum and instruction but are not entitled to all of the specially designed instruction or legal protections. These students may be covered under Section 504, which I describe later in this chapter.

A variety of assessment tools and strategies must be used when evaluating a student for special education eligibility, including information obtained from parents, classroom observations and assessments, and state assessments. Eligibility cannot be based on one instrument or score. The tests that are used must be "technically sound" for the area in which they are used. For example, an achievement test is not a valid measure of IQ. The tests must also not be culturally or racially biased.

Finally, it is very important that the assessment rule out "lack of appropriate instruction in reading or math" and limited English proficiency as reasons for a student's learning difficulties.

The regulations for IDEA specify the procedures, including mandatory timelines and notices, that must be followed to make certain that any student considered for special education has a comprehensive and individual multidisciplinary evaluation. It is extremely important that principals be aware of these timelines as well as the procedures for conducting evaluations.

Preventing Unnecessary Referrals and Special Education Identification

Overall, the students who receive special education are a very heterogeneous group. There are students with clear and medically defined disabilities as well as students who are experiencing significant learning difficulties but whose "disability" is less clearly defined. Research has shown over and over that decisions about which students have a "disability" in the second group can be extremely subjective.

Since the passage of the 1975 Education for All Handicapped Children's Act known as PL 94-142, the original special education law, the number and characteristics of students who have been identified to receive special education and related services have increased dramatically. For instance, the percentage of students identified with learning disabilities increased almost 300% since this group of students was included in the definitions, and the autism rates have increased over 400% in the past decade alone. As I noted earlier, federal law specifies 13 categories of disabilities that are eligible to receive special education. However, the vast majority of students in special education are classified in only four of those categories: learning disabilities, speech and language impairment, mild mental retardation, and emotional disturbance.

Box 1.3   Percentage of Students Receiving Special Education:*

All Disabilities	9%
Learning Disabilities	4%
Speech and Language Disabilities	2%
Mental Retardation	1%
Emotional Disturbance	1%
Multiple Disabilities	0.20%
Hearing Impairments	0.09%
Orthopedic Impairments	0.05%
Other Health Impairments	0.44**
Visual Impairments	0.07
Autism	0.34
Deaf-Blindness	0.00***
Traumatic Brain Injury	0.04

There is another category, Developmental Delay, that may be used by states for some students up to age nine; however, national statistics are not available.

---

*Percentage of the population of 6–22-year-olds in 2006.

**Can include students with attention deficit/hyperactivity disorder in some states.

***Number is too small to calculate.

SOURCE: www.ideadata.org

Research suggests that increased identification rates for some disabilities, such as autism and Asperger's syndrome as well as attention deficit/hyperactivity disorder, are due to new, more refined diagnostic criteria and research. In other categories such as learning disabilities and emotional disturbance, there is more evidence that the increases are a result of inadequate instruction in general education and failure to provide good behavior management and social skill development.

The vast majority—80% of students identified with learning disabilities, mild mental retardation, and emotional disturbance—is identified only after the students have been in school for several years and have a history of failure and behavior problems. Failure to progress in the curriculum is the symptom that most often prompts regular education teachers or parents to seek evaluations for special education. Those achievement difficulties are most often in reading, followed by math, and can be compounded by social and behavioral problems. Identification rates also differ across ages.

Research in special education has consistently demonstrated that disability classifications and labels do not explain poor achievement or determine which instruction the student needs to improve his or her learning. Elaborate diagnostic evaluations, including IQ tests, also do not result in a specific plan for instruction, and they are not sensitive enough to be able to monitor the effects of instruction. We also know that the earlier we, as educators, intervene with a learning or behavioral problem, the better the outcome. This research has led to a new way of conceptualizing learning disabilities as well as new IDEA policies that focus on prevention of learning difficulties and behavior problems.

Response to Intervention (RtI)

Response to Intervention (RtI), sometimes called Response to Instruction, is a new model for determining eligibility for special education, specifically for students suspected of having a learning disability. The central purpose of RtI is to rule out the referrals to special education of students who are not learning due to poor or inadequate instruction. RtI focuses on how a student responds to systematic and increasingly more intensive levels of instructional interventions that are implemented by general education teachers. The interventions are usually referred to as "tiers" and defined as follows:

Tier 1—High quality, evidence-based instruction provided to all students in the general education classroom and universal screening assessments to determine which students are at risk of not learning to read or for behavioral problems.

Tier 2—Small-group instruction provided by general educators to those students who need extra assistance in specific skill areas in which they are deficient. These interventions are time limited, perhaps six weeks or so, and students' progress is continually monitored.

Tier 3—Individualized and even more intensive instruction provided to students who fail to make satisfactory progress in Tier 2. In some models, moving to Tier 3 triggers evaluation for special education eligibility.

There are basically two RtI models. One type of model is referred to as "problem solving." These models typically involve schoolwide or grade-level teams that develop Tier 2 and Tier 3 instructional strategies for individual students. Many schools already have such teams, which are called such things as School Support Teams, Instructional

Support Teams, and so forth. Under RtI, the interventions proposed by the team to address a student's learning or behavior problem must be based on solid evidence, and the student's "response to" the intervention must be carefully monitored to ensure that the student is progressing.

A second model of RtI, sometimes called the "standard protocol," involves very specific instructional strategies applied for specific amounts of time at each tier. This model also requires careful monitoring of individual student progress.

Research using RtI has been conducted primarily in the area of early reading instruction with primary age students. Research has shown that RtI is a much more straightforward approach to identifying a student for special education, but requires skilled general education teachers who are able to deliver evidence-based instruction and precisely monitor student progress.

Learning disability groups and researchers recognize that the approach is better than the former "discrepancy" model, which required that students demonstrate a discrepancy between ability and achievement, sometimes referred to as standard deviations between IQ and achievement scores. However, there are a number of concerns about how well prepared general education teachers are to implement the procedures, and there is risk that some students who need special education may not receive it, or the students will not be identified in a timely manner.

Nevertheless, the RtI policy has been implemented because too many students are referred and found eligible for special education because of inadequate or inappropriate general education instruction. This has resulted in increased numbers of students being identified for special education, which has driven up costs and

> According to the National Association of State Directors of Special Education and the Council of Administrators of Special Education (CASE, 2006b), Tier 1 practices should be effective for an estimated 80%–85% of students, and Tier 2 interventions would likely address the achievement difficulties of another 13%–15% of the students. This means that only about 5% of the student population should be expected to move to Tier 3.

> Following are excellent sources for details about the IDEA:
>
> - Fuchs, D., & Deshler, D.D. (2007). What we need to know about responsiveness to intervention (and shouldn't be afraid to ask). *Learning Disabilities Research & Practice, 22*(2), 129–136.
> - U.S. Department of Education. (2004). *Building the legacy: IDEA 2004. Part B: Identification of specific learning disabilities.* Retrieved February 12, 2008, from http://idea.ed.gov/explore/view/p/,root,dynamic,Topical Brief,23

paperwork, not to mention the possibility of stigmatizing students with labels and lowered expectations.

Issues of stigma and low expectations are at the core of one of the other issues with special education eligibility: the disproportionate identification of minority students. African American males, in particular, have been overrepresented in special education for years, particularly in the categories of mild mental retardation and emotional disturbance.

Minority Students and Special Education Identification

One of the most difficult issues educators have faced over the years has been the overrepresentation of minority students in special education. While White students make up almost two thirds of all those receiving special education, over 20% of the students are African American and 14% are Hispanic. African American students are almost 3 times more likely to be classified as mentally retarded and about 1.5 times more likely to be classified as emotionally disturbed compared to White students.

Many studies have concluded that the problem results from a combination of bias in the referral and diagnostic evaluation process and the lack of appropriate general education instruction and support.

Both the U.S. Office of Civil Rights and the U.S. Department of Education have been concerned for a long time about the overidentification of African American and Hispanic students for special education. The procedures for determining eligibility for special education were intended to reduce inappropriate identification. The IDEA also includes some new provisions that are designed to reduce disproportionality.

Early Intervening Services (EIS)

The IDEA now permits a local school district to use up to 15% of the federal special education funds it receives to develop "early intervening services" for students in grades K–12. The EIS funds are to be used for students who are not currently identified as needing special education or related services, but who need additional academic and behavior support to succeed in general education and hopefully prevent special education identification.

Early intervening services can include professional development for teachers and other school staff on scientifically based academic and behavioral interventions and educational and behavioral evaluations, services, and supports. Districts that are identified as having "significant disproportionality" in identification, placement, or suspensions and expulsions are required to use the full 15% of the funds. How districts are designated as having "significant disproportionality" is determined by each state.

PROCEDURAL SAFEGUARDS—"THE LAW IN SPECIAL EDUCATION"

Procedural safeguards are the protections in IDEA that ensure that students with disabilities and their parents or guardians are meaningfully involved in all decisions related to the student's special education and that they have the right to seek a review of any decisions they think are appropriate. The procedural safeguards are grounded in the 5th and 14th Amendments of the U.S. Constitution, which guarantee that no person shall be deprived of life, liberty, or property without due process of the law.

The procedural safeguards in IDEA give parents and students the right to the following:

1. An independent educational evaluation (IEE) conducted by a qualified examiner who is not employed by the public agency responsible for the child's education. The parents can request an IEE if they disagree with the school's evaluation results, and in some cases, the district may have to pay for the IEE.

2. Notification of any action (in relation to the student's program) proposed by the school district. Written notice is required prior to the school's proposing to initiate or change the identification, evaluation, educational placement, or provisions in an IEP. In addition, the parents have the right to a written notice prior to the school district refusing to make such changes. The purpose of parental notification is to enable parents to fully participate in the special education process and to protect their child's rights.

3. Access to the student's entire educational record. This includes identification, evaluation, education placement documents, and documents related to the provisions of FAPE. If the parents request to see these documents, the school must comply within 45 days. However, the school must comply to the request prior to any meeting about the student's IEP or a due process hearing.

4. Mediation, resolution sessions, and due process hearings to resolve complaints.

5. Request that the student "stay put" in his or her current placement or program during any administrative or judicial proceeding

regarding a complaint. There are a few exceptions, which include when the school district and parents agree to remove the student from the current placement or if the student is a danger to himself or others.

6. An "interim alternative educational setting," which means a place where the student can receive special education services specified in his or her IEP after he or she has been suspended or removed from school for more than 10 school days due to misconduct. The student must be able to have access to the general education curriculum, make progress toward his or her IEP goals, and receive services to keep the misbehavior from reoccurring.

7. Unilaterally place the student in a private placement. The parents have a right to recover tuition from these unilateral private placements if the school district is determined to have failed to provide an appropriate education.

8. Due process hearings and the rights that go along with those hearings. For instance, parents have the right to be accompanied or advised by counsel, present evidence, cross-examine witnesses, and see evidence five days prior to a hearing; receive electronic findings of decisions; and have an open hearing. Parents have a right to have the child present at a due process hearing.

9. File a civil action to appeal a hearing decision. A civil action usually cannot be filed until all the administrative options have been exhausted.

10. Reasonable attorney's fees, if they are the prevailing party in an IDEA-related action.

Resolving Disputes

If parents disagree with the actions of the school related to their child or feel that the school did not follow correct procedures, the parents may use mediation, a resolution session, or a due process hearing to resolve the dispute.

Mediation is a voluntary and collaborative problem-solving process in which a trained, impartial party negotiates an agreement between the parent and school representatives. The mediator will facilitate discussion, encourage the open exchange of information, and assist parties in coming to a mutually agreeable solution. Mediation resolutions are legally binding written agreements, which are signed by both parties and enforceable in a state or federal court.

Resolution sessions are a step between mediation and a due process hearing. For a resolution session, a school district convenes a meeting between parents and relevant IEP team members to discuss a complaint and attempt to resolve it. There are strict timelines for when the meeting must be held and the issue resolved. If the complaint is settled through this process, both parties sign a legally binding agreement.

During a *due process hearing,* an impartial third party, a hearing officer, listens to both sides of the dispute between a parent and a school district, examines all issues, and settles the dispute. Parents have the right to request a due process hearing to contest identification, evaluation, placement, or the IEP, as well as to resolve procedural violations if they adversely affected the student's education. Very few—less than 3 per 10,000 students—proceed to a hearing, and most hearings are resolved in favor of the school district. Parents may file a civil action only after exhausting all other methods of dispute resolution.

Discipline and the IDEA

The IDEA requires that "disciplinary procedures applicable to children without disabilities may be applied to the child in the same manner and for the same duration as would be applied to children without disabilities," with three important exceptions:

- Services may not be stopped.
- The behavior must be addressed.
- The behavior must be linked to the student's disability.

The discipline procedures that must be followed for students with disabilities served under IDEA are part of the procedural safeguards. The IDEA does not prescribe discipline measures. It does require that during any pending administrative or judicial proceedings, a student "shall remain in the then current placement" unless the parents, state, and district agree otherwise. This is called the "stay put" provision.

The current IDEA discipline requirements were added in response to a U.S. Supreme Court decision, *Honig v. Doe* (1988), which determined that expelling a student with a disability was a change of placement that required a decision of the full IEP team. The ruling also noted that the "stay put" provision in the IDEA does not contain any exceptions, so that schools cannot unilaterally expel or indefinitely suspend a student with a disability.

Box 1.4   Basic Discipline Requirements Under the IDEA

- The student is entitled to IDEA benefits even if suspended or expelled.
- No student may be removed from school over 10 school days; schools may unilaterally use emergency suspension not to exceed 10 days.
- If the school wishes to enforce a long-term removal—over 10 school days—the school may use an Interim Alternative Placement (IAE) for up to 45 school days; repeated long-term suspensions are not allowed, and educational services must continue in the event of long-term suspension or expulsion.
- There are exceptions made for offenses involving drugs, weapons, and bodily injury.
- Seclusion or timeouts and in-school suspension may be used.
- Aversive techniques may be used if they are applied to any student and not just those with disabilities.
- The specific behaviors that are interfering with a student's learning or that of others must be explicitly addressed in the IEP.

For a student to be covered by the IDEA discipline procedures, the school must establish a link between a student's disability and behavior. This requires conducting a *manifestation determination* no later than 10 days following a suspension. The IEP team must be convened to determine whether the behavior is a result of or related to the student's disability and whether the student's IEP is appropriate.

Two questions must be answered during a manifestation determination: (a) Did the disability impair the student's ability to understand the impact and consequences of the behavior? (b) Did the disability impair the student's ability to control the behavior?

The IDEA discipline procedures also cover students who have not yet been determined to have a disability. If the school had knowledge that the student had a disability before the behavior event, then the school must conduct a manifestation determination and the "stay put" requirement applies.

OTHER IMPORTANT LAWS AFFECTING STUDENTS WITH DISABILITIES

There are several other laws that impact the education of students with disabilities. A principal should understand the requirements of these laws and policies and their intents.

Title I of the Elementary and Secondary Education Act—"No Child Left Behind"

Perhaps the best known policy in schools today is the No Child Left Behind Act (NCLB). One of the requirements of this law is that schools and districts be held accountable for achieving "Adequate Yearly Progress" (AYP) for several subgroups of students, one of which is students with disabilities. The NCLB extends the IDEA requirements that students with disabilities participate in all state and local assessments and have their scores reported both separately as well as part of the larger population of students and to be entitled to assessment accommodations and alternate assessments. Beyond the assessment and accountability requirements, NCLB regulations also call for students with disabilities to be instructed in the same grade-level content standards that have been established for all other students.

The requirement that students with disabilities be fully included in state standards ensures that these students will benefit from the programs and resources implemented in schools that are designed to increase student achievement. The NCLB and IDEA policies address the historic problems in special education of low expectations for students with disabilities, isolated IEP goals, and special education instruction that is overwhelmingly focused on low level skills. In the past, students with disabilities were exempted from state or local assessments or had their scores "hidden" or not counted with the scores of the general population of students. There also was no accountability for results, and the IEPs became more and more separated from general education curriculum and instruction.

Both the IDEA and NCLB have changed the expectations for how students with IEPs are to be included in state standards, assessments, and accountability. In the next section, I discuss more about this new approach of standards-based instruction for students with disabilities. Before considering how to implement this new model for special education, it is important to review some of the requirements that specifically pertain to assessment accountability and students with disabilities.

The IDEA and NCLB both demand that all students with disabilities be included in assessments and that assessment participation of students with disabilities is to be included in the 95% calculation.

Students with disabilities may participate in assessments in any of the following ways:

- Assessment with no accommodations.
- Assessment with accommodations.
- Alternate assessment based on grade level achievement standards.

- Alternate assessment based on *modified* achievement standards ("2% Rule").
- Alternate assessment based on *alternate* achievement standards ("1% Rule").

Alternate Achievement Standards and Assessments

Under NCLB, students with "significant cognitive disabilities" can be assessed using alternate achievement standards. An alternate achievement standard is "an expectation of performance that differs in complexity from a grade-level achievement standard" (U.S. Department of Education, 2005, p.20) that must be aligned with a state's academic content standards. However, an alternate achievement standard can reflect a prerequisite skill rather than grade-level skills. The IEP team determines which students should be assessed using an alternate assessment and which students will be assessed against "alternate achievement standards." However, the number of "proficient" scores of these students that can be counted in the district or state level AYP calculations is limited to 1% of the students assessed.

States may also develop *modified* achievement standards for a limited group of students with disabilities and develop alternate assessments based on those achievement standards. The states and districts may include up to 2% of the proficient scores from these assessments in determining AYP.

Modified achievement standards must be challenging, but they may be less difficult than grade-level academic achievement standards. They must be aligned with a state's academic content standards for the grade in which a student is enrolled. This means that only the *achievement* standards are modified, not the content that is taught to the students.

IEP teams need to follow specific guidelines and justify any decision to assess a student using a modified achievement standard. They must also apply the following criteria:

- There must be objective evidence demonstrating that the student's disability has precluded the student from achieving grade-level proficiency.
- The student's progress in response to appropriate instruction, including special education and related services, indicates to the IEP team that the student will not achieve grade-level proficiency within the year covered by his or her IEP. The IEP team must use multiple measures of the student's progress over time in making this determination.
- The student's IEP must include goals that are based on the academic content standards for the grade in which the student is enrolled.

Another important policy area has to do with the legal issues surrounding assessing students with disabilities. As noted earlier, NCLB and IDEA require states to provide both accommodations and alternate forms of assessments. In addition, several court cases have influenced considerations regarding a student's participation in general education assessments.

LEGAL ISSUES AND ASSESSING STUDENTS WITH DISABILITIES

In the case of *Board of Education of the Hendrick Hudson School District v. Rowley* (1982), the court held that a school district has an obligation to provide accommodations to support students' performance based on state standards. The *Brookhart v. Illinois State Board of Education* (1983) case concerned students with disabilities who did not pass their graduation tests and were denied high school diplomas. The court ruled that an inability to learn material cannot be overlooked in granting diplomas. However, the court also noted that Section 504 and special education law require that a test be valid and suited for its intended purpose and appropriate for the group being tested. Another leading court decision on test-based graduation requirements, *Debra P. v. Turlington* (1981), concerned Black students who had attended illegally segregated schools in Florida and were failing the state competency exams. The court ruled that the state could not withhold diplomas until the students had an opportunity to attend integrated schools and an opportunity to learn what was being assessed.

More recently, in *Rene v. Reed* (2001), a federal court of appeals upheld Indiana's right to restrict the type of accommodations permitted on the high school exit examination if the accommodations would invalidate the results of the assessment. In Oregon, the state and advocates reached a settlement in a case alleging that the statewide assessment program discriminated against learning-disabled students. A blue-ribbon panel was convened and made the following recommendations to improve the test: increase the numbers of allowable accommodations and use them as part of the student's instruction, and make available both alternate scoring procedures and alternate assessments to students with learning disabilities for any component of an assessment that is essential to receipt of a diploma.

Finally, a federal district court in *Chapman et al. v. California Department of Education*

> Want to learn more about assessing students with disabilities? Visit the National Center on Educational Outcomes Web site: http://cehd.umn.edu/nceo

(2002) halted the administration of the California High School Exit Exam. The court determined that students with disabilities must be permitted to take the exam with any accommodation or modification specified on their IEPs for testing or for general classroom instruction. Furthermore, if the IEP calls for an alternate assessment, one must be provided for the high school assessment as well.

OTHER FEDERAL DISABILITY LAWS

There are several other federal laws that provide important protections or services to children and adults with disabilities in public schools. Two major civil rights laws are Section 504 of the 1973 Vocational Rehabilitation Act and the 1990 Americans with Disabilities Act (ADA). Section 504 prohibits discrimination of persons with disabilities in all federally supported programs. It is broader than IDEA both in terms of which students are covered under the law. The ADA is a comprehensive civil rights law that protects persons with disabilities in employment, public services and public accommodations, transportation, and telecommunications. Table 1.1 presents a comparison of key features of the three laws.

In addition, several programs established under the Social Security Act that are administered by individual states are also available to some students with disabilities. These include Medicaid (medical insurance), State Children's Health Insurance Program (medical insurance), and Supplemental Security Income, which provides payments to families of children under 18 who meet specific criteria of physical or mental impairment.

UNDERSTANDING THE DIFFERENCES AMONG FEDERAL, STATE, AND LOCAL SPECIAL EDUCATION REQUIREMENTS

A frequent statement made by principals, teachers, and parents is "The law requires that we do this!" What I have just described are the federal policies that govern special education. Each state has its own set of rules that interpret federal requirements. In addition, local districts must develop policies and procedures that are consistent with federal and state laws but which may also have additional requirements. How special education is delivered in the schools represents a complex mix of federal and special education laws and regulations and local policies, practices, and tradition. Sometimes procedures have developed out of lawsuits or

Table 1.1 Educators Guide to American with Disabilities Act (ADA): A Comparison

	ADA	Section 504	Part B of Individuals with Disabilities Education Act (IDEA)
Definition of disability	An individual with a disability is one who has a physical or mental impairment, has a record of such an impairment, or is regarded by others as having such an impairment. The impairment must substantially limit a major life activity.	Section 504 is nearly identical to ADA.	A child age 3–21 who has been evaluated according to IDEA regulations and has mental retardation, a hearing impairment including deafness, a speech or language impairment, a visual impairment including blindness, emotional disturbance, an orthopedic impairment, autism, traumatic brain injury, another health impairment, a specific learning disability, deaf-blindness, or multiple disabilities *and who because of the disability needs special education and related services.* In some states, children between ages 3–9 may be identified as having developmental delays. Children who require only "related services" and not special education are not eligible under the IDEA.
Eligibility	To be covered under the law, a person must meet the ADA's definition of disability (and be qualified for the program, service, or job, in the case of employment).	Section 504 is the same as the ADA. Students who have a disability that does not have an adverse impact on their ability to learn but may require special accommodation to access education may have individual accommodation plans.	A student must have one of the disabilities covered in the law's definition and must need special education and related services.
Funding	There is no funding through the ADA.	There is no funding through Section 504.	Funds are provided to state education agencies that must "flow" the funds to local districts. States may devise their own formula for allocating federal (and state) special education funds.

SOURCE: Adapted from Section 504 and ADA. *Promoting Student Access: A Resource Guide for Educators.* Council of Administrators of Special Education (CASE) 2006a.

compliance monitoring, and all districts and states have their own history for how special education is provided. Federal law holds state education agencies accountable for ensuring that the basic provisions and intents of the IDEA are met. The states delegate responsibility to their local districts to implement all legal procedures and rely on local districts to set policies and monitor practices. This delegation of responsibility results in variability across states, local districts, and schools in terms of how eligibility is determined, where and how special education and related services are provided, and what procedures must be followed.

Now that I have discussed the basic structure of special education policy, I turn in the next section to the features of high-quality special education programs. Creating a quality special education program requires that a principal know much more than the basic legal policies and procedures.

Creating Quality Special Education

The Foundations

Key Ideas for Section II

A high-quality special education program has four features:

- ➢ Students with disabilities have meaningful access to the general education curriculum.
- ➢ Students with disabilities are fully included in all assessment and accountability systems.
- ➢ Classroom and school environments promote positive behavior among all students.
- ➢ Strong parent and family communication and collaboration are present.

A NEW MODEL OF SPECIAL EDUCATION

Federal policies are increasingly blurring the lines between general and special education. This is most apparent when it comes to ensuring that every student with a disability has the opportunity to access and progress in the general education curriculum and that the student's IEP directly refers to that curriculum. This is a new way of thinking about special education. The traditional model of special education viewed students with disabilities in relative isolation from general education. That is, a child was assessed, his or her learning strengths and deficits were identified, and individual goals, objectives, and strategies were devised to meet the deficits. These evaluations and IEP goals typically were conducted in isolation from the general education curriculum and expectations. The IEP goals focused on short-term and discrete skill deficits, and IEPs were often a collection of isolated skill objectives that led to isolated instruction. A student's program may have been individualized, but it was also separated from the larger scope and sequence of the curriculum.

The new model of special education, which I illustrate in Figure 2.1, is one in which special education is defined as a set of services and supports existing in a school and designed to help each student make progress in the general education curriculum. In this model, the special education students are represented within the rectangle. As you examine this figure, you can see that in some instances, there may not be a marked difference between a general education student and a student receiving special education. Yet, the latter students are entitled to IEPs. So let's think about how that IEP should be developed.

In the model, every student's IEP should be based on an assessment that indicates where he or she is situated in the scope and sequence of the general education curriculum. That is, the IEP teams needs to know what skills, concepts, and constructs the student has mastered. The team also needs to identify the accommodations, supports, and services are needed to help a student learn the content. These can include specific instructional strategies, technologies, or special materials. How the student's progress will be monitored must also be specified. In addition, special education may supplement the general education curriculum by providing instruction in specific skill areas not addressed in the general education curriculum, such as social and behavioral skills, functional living skills, or other access skills, such as learning strategies, but these are not intended to take the place of instruction in the content of the general education curriculum. All of these decisions are individualized and start from an understanding of the expectations of the general education curriculum and what is required to help the student access that curriculum.

ACCESS TO THE GENERAL EDUCATION CURRICULUM

Using Figure 2.1 as a guide, IEP planning for each child begins with the assumption that the student will be taught the grade-level subject matter content as defined by the general education curriculum. This expectation exists regardless of the setting or environment in which the student is

Figure 2.1   Special Education: A "Curriculum Continuum"

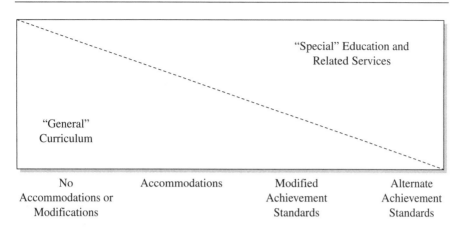

"Special" Education and
Related Services

"General"
Curriculum

| No
Accommodations or
Modifications | Accommodations | Modified
Achievement
Standards | Alternate
Achievement
Standards |

being educated. For some students, such as those receiving only speech and language services, no changes may be necessary to the curriculum or the instruction that is provided within the general classroom. The indicator arrow on Figure 2.2a shows students such as these positioned on the curriculum continuum. Their IEP goals may be solely in speech and language and rest in the upper diagonal.

The next level of the access continuum assumes that instructional and assessment accommodations will be made, but that the student will be expected to learn all of the grade-level curriculum content like his or her peers in general education. Neither content nor achievement standards are changed. As Figure 2.2b illustrates, a greater portion of these students' educational programs may involve specialized educational goals and related services. The specially designed instruction may also focus on accommodations, such as additional intensive instruction, assistive or instructional technology, and strategies for learning designed to help the student's general education content and instruction.

Before I discuss the continuum for students held to "modified" or "alternate" achievement standards, it is important to differentiate between accommodations and modifications.

UNDERSTANDING ACCOMMODATIONS

An accommodation does not change the content of instruction or the performance expectations. The student is expected to learn substantially the same information as the rest of the class and work toward the same content and performance standards as do the other students. An accommodation is intended to offset the impact of a student's disability so that the student can both learn the same material as his or her peers without

Figure 2.2   Special Education: A "Curriculum Continuum"

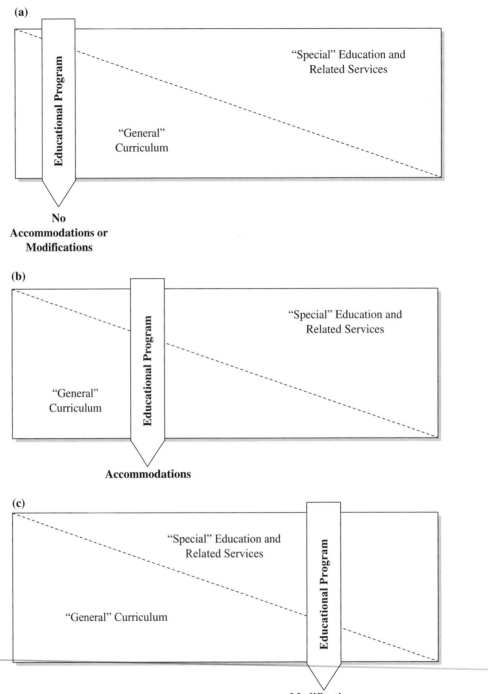

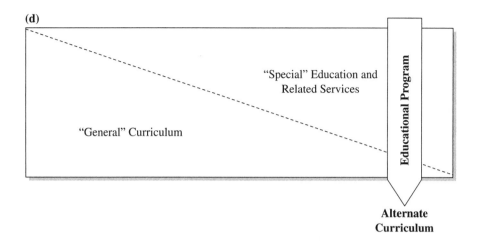

disabilities as well as demonstrate what he or she knows on the same assessments given to the other students.

Accommodations may involve changes to the sequence in which material is presented or the timelines on which a student is expected to learn curriculum information: for example, allowing a student more time to complete an assignment or test, allocating more time for a student to complete a reading assignment, or changing a student's setting to a quieter place. Often, accommodations involve use of certain technology, ranging from simple (e.g., pencil grips or large print books) to more complex (e.g., calculators, spell checkers, personal digital assistants, and laptop computers).

Accommodations also can include providing a student with additional opportunities to practice or apply specific skills or concepts using a variety of materials or situations. An accommodation might entail providing individualized or small-group instruction in a specific skill area to help a student master an important concept or skill set.

Assessment accommodations are intended to be used as part of instruction. Thus, students should not encounter an accommodation for the first time when they take an assessment. Among the crucial roles the principal can play is to make sure that IEP teams are aware that an accommodation does not alter major learning outcomes in the curriculum, and the accommodations must reflect the needs of the student, not just what is convenient or readily available. Also, instructional accommodations can go beyond those that have been approved by the state for use on assessments. The principal also can ensure that the IEP team includes a teacher or other member with a deep understanding of the curriculum and what content students are expected to learn at each grade level. This individual can help determine whether a particular accommodation could alter a core content expectation. Finally, principals need to ensure that teachers can access a full array of accommodations for individual students.

Assessment Accommodations

States have policies that specify which accommodations are permitted on the state assessment and which students are allowed which accommodations. These policies differ across states but most fall into five categories (see Box 2.1):

Box 2.1   Types of Assessment Accommodations

- *Setting*—Change the test location to allow a child to take the test in a small group or individually.
- *Timing*—Allow extended time or take frequent test breaks.
- *Scheduling*—Allow testing over several days or administer only during a specific time.
- *Presentation*—Change the format, use an assistive device such as a reader, or provide computer assistance.
- *Response*—Change how a student responds, such as using a scribe, recorder, or computer.

Can a Student Have Any Type of Accommodation?

The IEP team decides which assessment accommodations a student with a disability requires. The accommodations should be provided in instruction as well as during the assessment. However, not every accommodation that an individual student needs in instruction may be permitted during an assessment, and not every accommodation is necessarily relevant to instruction. For example, in a high stakes test, a student with a disability might take the assessment in a quiet room with extended time to minimize distractions. However, a short spelling test or other classroom assessment might be given with the rest of the class if the teacher and student believe it will not interfere with performance.

Some accommodations may invalidate an assessment, which is why some states restrict the types of accommodations allowed on different tests. For example, having someone read a test that is assessing a student's ability to decode text could invalidate the construct (e.g., decoding print) that is being measured. Similarly, using a calculator on an assessment of mathematical computation could invalidate that test. However, reading a test that measures how well a student comprehends text might not change the construct, and the use of a calculator will not necessarily invalidate a math reasoning test.

The scores of students who take a high stakes assessment with a non-approved accommodation may not "count". Under NCLB, that score will count as below Basic.

Do Accommodations Affect Student Test Scores?

There has also been a great deal of research conducted on the effects of assessment accommodations on test scores, but most of it is inconclusive.

We do know, for example, that the most common accommodations offered to students with disabilities are extended time and multiple testing sessions. But most often a student receives more than one accommodation on an assessment, such as having more time and taking the test in a small group or private setting. Some research that has been conducted in very controlled studies suggests that the impacts of accommodations can be positive or negative depending on an individual student. This means that an accommodation that improves one student's performance may actually detract from another student's performance. Other research has suggested that for some accommodations, such as extended time, many students with disabilities who receive this accommodation do not actually end up needing it because they can finish the test in the standard amount of time. This is why it's important for IEP teams to understand how an accommodation might impact assessment as well as to make certain that the student knows how to use the accommodation.

Modifications

In contrast to accommodations, modifications change the expectations for what a student may be expected to actually learn. Under the NCLB, some students with disabilities may be held to "modified achievement" standards, but they are still expected to be instructed in grade-level subject matter content. Students in this category may have a considerable portion of their program as specially designed instruction. There may need to be adjustments to some of the topics covered, the instructional sequences or timelines, or the instructional strategies employed. Modifications can involve use of different curriculum materials, such as vocabulary-controlled textbooks. Teachers attempt to reduce the curriculum load. Teachers also must spend more instructional time focused on foundational skills by identifying and focusing on the critical skills and concepts in a unit of instruction. For instance, changing a textbook or curricular materials can be an accommodation or a modification. The test is how it changes the standard.

Modifications must be made with caution. They often reduce a student's opportunity to learn the critical knowledge, skills, and concepts in certain subject matter, which in turn will affect his or her future ability to learn more difficult content. The effect of modifications can be to "dumb down" the curriculum to such an extent that the student no longer has access to the same curriculum as the rest of the class. For example, off-grade-level texts may reduce demands for reading and language skills, but they very likely present very different concepts, vocabulary, and other key skills. Thus, it may be necessary to use accommodations such as audiotaped tests, calculators, and so forth, in some domains, and vocabulary–controlled materials in other situations. This allows a student access to the more cognitively complex content while accommodating skills, such as literacy, that may be weak. The student will also need specific instruction in those deficient skill areas.

Curricular modifications have both long- and short-term implications and need to be carefully designed by the IEP team.

> See the following for an excellent source on how to adjust curriculum standards: Nolet, V., & McLaughlin, M. J. (2005). *Accessing the general curriculum: Including students with disabilities in standards-based reform* (2nd ed.). Thousand Oaks, CA: Corwin Press.

Box 2.2   Questions to Guide Modifications

- *Will we teach the same content but lower the performance expectation?*

  Here the decision is to provide an opportunity for the student to be exposed to all of the same knowledge and instruction that is provided to the typical student, but to reduce the expectations of what the student will have to demonstrate. This decision is very much related to teaching less content but assumes that the student should receive instruction in all of what is taught, but he or she will only be expected to learn less.

- *Will we teach less content?*

  There are a variety of ways to make this modification: the student learns fewer objectives or curricular benchmarks, the student completes shorter units or parts of a unit, the student reads fewer pages or paragraphs, or the student participates in shorter lessons or parts of lessons.

> • *Will we set alternative goals?*
>
> As I previously noted, every student could have some IEP goals that reflect very specific skills or knowledge that is required to address the impacts of the disability. However, with respect to alternative curriculum goals, I refer to those few students who are working toward an individualized set of instructional goals or objectives based on alternate achievement standards.

Finally, a totally individualized set of IEP goals based on alternate achievement standards may be defined for very few students. As Figure 2.2d shows, when a student is receiving instruction based on alternate achievement standards, the IEP is individualized and almost the entire education program involves special education. The students are still expected to receive instruction in the subject matter content defined by state content standards; however, that content is typically significantly individualized.

Many teachers and principals find it challenging to provide every student with a disability access to the general education grade-level curriculum, particularly when these students are typically many years behind their peers in terms of achievement. As a result, they attempt to focus instruction on the lowest skill area. Achieving access means much more than placing a student in a general education classroom or "exposing" a student to content. Providing real access requires deep understanding of curriculum assessment and instruction. It also requires that special and general education teachers collaborate in new ways and that special education programs and services at the school level be more flexible than ever before.

Box 2.3   Example of an Alternate Achievement Standard

General English Language Arts Grade 5 Standard:

Determine the meaning of unfamiliar words using context clues.

Alternate Achievement Standard:

Given a spoken word, the student will identify the correct photograph from a group of two with 80% accuracy and 80% independence.

Box 2.4   Examples of Accommodations and Modifications

Accommodations do not change the content or performance expectations. They may change the sequence in which information is presented, or they may entail differentiated instruction. Examples can include the following:

- Sign language
- Braille materials
- Recorded books
- Adaptive technology
- Content enhancements such as advance organizers and study guides
- Scribes or tape recorders instead of pencil and paper
- Additional opportunities for practice
- Additional examples or applications of skills or concepts

Modifications may involve changes to performance expectations, topics taught, curriculum sequences, or the type of instruction delivered. They do not change curriculum standards toward which a student works. Examples can include the following:

- Out-of-level texts
- Materials adjusted for reading level
- Fewer pages in a reading assignment
- Fewer problems in a homework assignment
- Fewer steps in a problem-solving activity
- Alternative expectations in a group assignment
- Fewer or simpler goals or objectives
- Skills instruction instead of content instruction

DEVELOPING STANDARDS-BASED IEPS

The IDEA has required since 1997 that students with disabilities have access to the general education curriculum. This requirement, as well as the NCLB regulations that call for all students but those with significant cognitive disabilities to be instructed in grade-level subject matter, have created a movement toward creating "standards-based IEPs."

As I previously noted, IEP teams in the past often developed parallel programs and separate educational services for students with disabilities. IEP goals traditionally focused on identifying specific skill deficits and remedying those deficits. Now IEP teams are being asked to determine *how* students with disabilities will access and make progress in the general education curriculum. And, since state grade-level content standards define the general education curriculum, it is reasonable that these standards should drive the IEP planning process.

Using state standards as the framework for an IEP is a vastly different approach from what has traditionally been followed in special education. Before the introduction of a standards-based approach, the IEP process started with a focus on the skills the child needed to learn with little reference to grade level expectations or curriculum. The emphasis would most often be on the child's acquisition of basic skills unrelated to what was being taught in the general education classroom.

A Decision-Making Process for Developing Standards-Based IEPs

As a principal, you might ask, "Why do I need all of this information about IEP development?" There are three reasons. As the instructional leader of a school

1. You must understand the critical role of the IEP in the instruction of students with disabilities.

2. You are responsible for ensuring that these students are held to high expectations and receive a high-quality curriculum.

3. You are accountable for improving the performance of all students in your building.

By now you know that the IEP is the centerpiece of planning a student's special education services or supports. The first step in the planning process is determining a student's Present Level of Educational Performance (PLEP) based on results of multidisciplinary evaluation data, statewide assessments, and classroom performance information. Regarding grade-level content, analyze **what** and **how** students are required to learn. Identify the gaps in key skills, concepts, and understanding between the grade-level expectations and the student's actual performance. Then the IEP team must set a *nnual goals* that directly relate to specific standards that students will be expected to learn and which focus on essential content knowledge and skills.

There are three basic phases in assessing a student's PLEP:

Phase 1—Identify the critical, enduring knowledge associated with the general curriculum that all students will learn (usually based on state and district standards).

Phase 2—Analyze the key knowledge and skills that a competent individual uses to perform tasks associated with that knowledge. This step is generally analogous to the process of task analysis familiar to many special educators. However, the work I am talking about here is *not* the same as the highly detailed analysis that IEP teams often conduct and that frequently results in goals and objectives focused on small subcomponents of basic skills.

Phase 3—Analyze the individual child's use of key learning processes and strategies.

IEP Goals

In addition to general curricular goals, IEPs must include any additional skills and knowledge areas beyond the general curriculum to be addressed through special education or related services. These goals will also need to be specified. Important questions for setting IEP goals include those shown in Box 2.5.

You should now see that access to the general education curriculum represents a complex set of decisions based on information about how well a student is currently performing in the general education curriculum as well as knowledge of the expectations for that student's performance in future years. In other words, what does the student need to know and be able to do by the end of elementary and middle school or by the time he or she is a young adult? Also required is a discussion of the implications of modifying or changing the curriculum. Remember, test results will not improve if students with disabilities do not have an opportunity to learn the material that is being assessed.

**Box 2.5   Questions to Guide the Standards-Based
              IEP Goals**

1. What will typical students be expected to do (math, science, reading, PE, and so on) during the time frame addressed by the IEP (this grading period, semester, year)?

   Usually you will want goals, objectives, and standards to define the student performances expected. Examples include being able to read specific text independently and answer questions, being able to accurately estimate size and measurement in a variety of daily situations, and being able to write a minimum of four paragraphs that logically develop an idea while conforming to rules of grammar and punctuation.

2. How is the target student currently performing in these areas?

   Look at classroom evidence regarding the key areas as well as input from parents, teachers, and other team members. The idea is to decide where the student falls on a continuum of competence on the standards or broad curriculum goals as well as skills they use for learning.

3. In what ways are the student's disabilities impacting the performance?

   In addition to specific skill deficits such as in reading or math, educational assessments should consider such things as improving attention or focus, memory, organizational skills, and communication, as well as other learning processes.

4. What accommodations and supports will the student need to offset the impact of the disability?

   For example, determine whether they will need memory aids, communication assistance, specific organizational strategies, more intensive instruction in certain areas, and so forth.

Box 2.6   A Real-Life Example of How Special and General Education Teachers Provide Access

In Westlake School District (not its real name), special and general education teachers have a history of collaborative planning and teaching. Originally, this was done to promote inclusion or the education of students with disabilities in general education classrooms. The district had provided professional development to both general and special education teachers in coteaching models and collaborative consultation. But, as the district implemented new content standards and tough new local and state assessments, the focus moved to ensuring that all students accessed the curricular standards. Students with disabilities were not just in the general education classrooms; they were learning core and essential knowledge and skills. A typical scenario in one of the district's middle schools follows:

Ms. Austin, a special educator, is assigned to the sixth-grade team. She meets regularly with the team to discuss issues related to the curriculum and other team issues. However, Ms. Austin also meets individually with each of the content teachers on the team to discuss in depth the units of instruction that will be covered during a grading period. Ms. Austin's conversations go something like this: "Basically, we talk about what they are planning to cover in the next grading period. In particular, we review the key concepts and the standards that will be addressed. The [content] teacher discusses the essential knowledge or skills that he or she wants every kid to really learn. I know that my job is to help the students with IEPs and 504 plans learn that. I focus my instruction and support on those areas. . . . We both agree that not everything that goes on in the class is of equal value. We need to focus our time and the kids' efforts on the standards that matter."

In one of the district's elementary schools, the special education teachers talk about loading up on planning time with the general education teachers at the beginning of the year and before each marking period. The principal finds time, using substitutes and creative scheduling, to allow for the special and general education teachers to meet to discuss the critical curriculum goals that should be the focus of the intensive support and instruction.

> Planning and communication during the grading period happen
> "on the fly" or in class, unless there is a specific problem. "We don't
> need regularly scheduled time to meet since we already understand
> what each of us is to be focusing on. We can debrief and keep on
> track on an ongoing basis."

PROMOTING POSITIVE BEHAVIOR OR
HOW TO AVOID THE DISCIPLINE PROBLEM

Probably nothing creates as much anxiety, frustration, and overall confusion for principals as the discipline procedures that apply to students
who receive special education. While it is important that principals
understand the origins of current legal requirements related to discipline
and students with disabilities, it is even more important that a school
leader understand how to create a schoolwide system of *positive behavioral supports* for managing the array of disciplinary events that might be
encountered in a school.

Much of the responsibility for anticipating and managing behavioral
problems of individual students rests with the IEP team. If the team antic-
ipates that behavior might be an issue for a student, it must analyze the
causes and consequences of the behavior as well as develop specific intervention plans. Generally, there are two areas that must be addressed in
developing the IEP:

1. The strengths of the child and the concerns of the parents for
   enhancing the education of their child, and the results of the initial evaluation or most recent evaluation of the student.

2. In the case of a student whose behavior impedes his or her learning or that of others, the IEP team must consider strategies including *positive behavioral interventions* and *supports* that address that
   behavior.

POSITIVE BEHAVIORAL INTERVENTIONS
AND SUPPORTS

In recent years, the focus on managing behavior of students has shifted
from reactive responses such as discipline procedures to prevention. An

A good source for understanding Positive Behavioral Interventions and Supports is http://www .pbis.org

evidence-based model referred to as Positive Behavioral Interventions and Supports (PBIS) is an evidence-based model for both preventing behavioral problems as well as intervening if such problems occur.

What Is PBIS?

PBIS is based on a three-tiered model of interventions that emphasizes prevention, active instruction aimed at improving social behaviors, using data to make decisions about individual students and programs, using research-validated strategies, and involving entire systems within and outside the school.

The three tiers include the following: (a) prevention strategies designed to reduce or eliminate new problems as well as the serious events among a small number of students, (b) specific attention to teaching appropriate behavioral and social skills, and (c) careful analysis of individual student behaviors and monitoring of overall progress.

- Emphasis on prevention—There are three levels of prevention in the PBIS framework: preventing the initiation of problem behaviors or preventing the escalation or severity of the behavior.
  - *Primary prevention*—The goal is to decrease the number of new behavior problems or disciplinary events in the school through use of schoolwide and classwide behavior management strategies and better instructional practices. Examples of schoolwide or classwide strategies are as follows: a common approach to discipline, a small number of clear expectations for behavior, uniform consequences for infractions, and training all staff and students in the expectation.
  - *Secondary prevention*—The goal is to reduce the number of students who demonstrate behavioral issues that may become serious problems. Interventions at this level are usually more specialized and focus on small groups of students. The interventions can include counseling, conflict resolution strategies, social skills training, anger management, and similar specialized programs. In addition, many of the students who need secondary prevention strategies are at risk of school failure and may need intensive academic support.

o *Tertiary prevention*—This level of intervention is highly specialized and is targeted toward reducing the number, frequency, and severity of behavioral incidents among a small number of students with serious behavior and emotional difficulties. Interventions are almost always designed by a team, including behavioral specialists, and are highly tailored to the individual. These students typically have IEPs and Behavioral Intervention Plans or BIPs (see Box 2.7).

- Improving social behaviors—Attempts to manage or correct problem behavior are more effective when they are accompanied by a systematic approach that supports positive behaviors. Research with PBIS has demonstrated that this approach includes the following: (a) promoting academic success and a feeling of efficacy among students and teachers; in other words, students believe that they can achieve and learn and teachers believe that they are effective in managing their classrooms and helping children learn; (b) promoting consistent classroom and school routines and expectations about behavior and civility; and (c) making clear to students what exactly is expected in various situations and providing opportunities to practice and demonstrate to students the specific social expectations.

- Using data to make decisions—In the area of behavior, Functional Behavioral Assessments (FBAs) are central to developing behavioral interventions at the secondary and tertiary levels (see Box 2.7).

Box 2.7   Functional Behavioral Assessment (FBA)

An FBA is a team process that involves the following:

- Collecting specific information about a student's behavior, what appeared to prompt the behavior, and the consequences.
- Developing hypotheses about what might be causing certain behaviors or maintaining the behaviors.
- Developing individualized behavioral intervention plans (BIPs) that use the assessment information to develop strategies that focus on the social and personal strengths of the student (such as family or peer networks, abilities, or interests)

(Continued)

(Continued)

and at the same time make the problem behavior ineffective or inefficient (in other words, eliminate the payoff to the student or make the behavior irrelevant).

- Understanding that BIPs will only be effective if they are developed in a collaborative structure so that all individuals—specialists, teachers, the principal, parents, and the student—clearly understand what the interventions are and accept responsibility for ensuring that the specific strategies are implemented.
- Monitoring the effects of the intervention; too often a BIP is implemented and no one takes responsibility for monitoring if the strategies are being implemented as intended or if the student's behavior improves.

Box 2.8   A Behavioral Intervention Plan

A Behavioral Intervention Plan (BIP) takes the observations and information obtained in a Functional Behavioral Assessment (FBA) and turns them into a plan for managing a student's behavior. A BIP may include ways to change the environment to keep a behavior from starting in the first place, provide positive reinforcement to promote good or coping behaviors, identify ways to avoid reinforcing bad behavior, and provide supports for learning and negotiating school so that a student will not be driven to act out because of frustration or fatigue.

The IDEA requires that when a student with a disability is removed from a current placement for more than 10 days, regardless of whether the behavior is a manifestation of the disability, the student must have an FBA and a BIP designed to address the behavior violation so that it does not recur.

A Sample BIP

Behavior impacting learning: abusive verbal outbursts, head down on desk, excessive talking, getting out of seat.

It impedes learning: because the student is unavailable for learning while experiencing the aforementioned behaviors, and the teacher is distracted along with the other students.

Estimate of current severity of behavior problem: mild to moderate.

Current frequency/intensity/duration of behavior: daily head down and talking; weekly verbal outbursts.

Current predictors for behavior: avoidance of frustrating learning situations, unexpected change in routine, projects that demand effort or are not immediately understood, too much stimulation at the same time, teacher demands to repeat a task, unstructured activity, teasing by peers.

What student should do instead of this behavior: express verbally to an adult if he or she does not understand a task, feels anxious, angry, or overstimulated, develop self-regulatory relaxation techniques.

Supports for the student using the problem behavior: adults remove the student from the class or frustrating situations; peers give attention to the student.

Behavioral goals/objectives related to this plan: development of age-appropriate coping and social skills, anger management, and self-regulatory skills, and development of appropriate verbal communication. Provide curriculum accommodation.

Teaching strategies for new behavior instruction: intervening with positive replacement behaviors, anticipating and preventing the antecedents causing the behavior, ignoring inappropriate behavior whenever possible but immediately rewarding all appropriate behavior. *By:* Name staff. *Frequency:* all the time until a new desired behavior is well established.

Environmental structure and supports, time/space/materials/ interactions: a designated "safe place" for establishment of self-regulatory coping mechanisms, acknowledgement by adults to allow the student his or her "space" and time to "regroup," and seating close to teacher, but allowing the student space to "spread out" to avoid confrontation with fellow students. Adult support is needed during any group or social interaction or activity by engaging in role playing and social skills training or stories, or to keep the student on task with the activity at hand.

Reinforcers/rewards: a reward system, with a foundation based on a motivator (e.g., computer games), to be developed by parents

(Continued)

(Continued)

and teachers. Aversive, negative disciplinary techniques will only exacerbate undesired behaviors. Upon resistance to a task, allow student to "regroup" and then readjust the task with flexibility in achieving a goal of completion, immediately rewarding any compliance to finish the task. *By:* Name staff. *Frequency:* all the time until a new desired behavior is well established.

Reactive strategy to employ if behavior occurs again: avoid power struggles, allow the student to regroup in his or her "safe place," validate the student's feelings and encourage the child to express verbally his or her frustration, anger, anxiety, and so forth.

Monitoring results and communication—options: daily and weekly reports in "Weekly Planner" by teachers. The reward system will be "tracked" in writing by teachers and given to special education staff biweekly. All staff involved will meet biweekly or more often as needed until team members have established that the student is adequately supported and is developing the desired appropriate behaviors.

SOURCE: Adapted from http://specialchildren.about.com

Box 2.9   A Study of a Positive Behavioral Support System

A recent 2-year study was conducted by Nelson, Martella, and Marchand-Martella (2002) in seven elementary schools in which positive behavior support systems were implemented. The seven study schools were then compared to 28 other elementary schools in the district in a number of areas. Each school went through the following phases:

- School faculty identified specific problems and gaps in programs and services.
- A leadership team was created to guide the process.
- Schoolwide practices were assessed and interventions designed and approved by faculty consensus that addressed schoolwide organizational practices, schoolwide classroom management practices, and individualized BIPs.

- Progress was monitored through the use of office referrals and other discipline data, teacher surveys, and interviews.
- A schoolwide assessment addressed issues related to space and scheduling.
- Space issues that contributed to behavior problems included playground areas that were out of view and not supervised and where prohibited activities, including bullying, would occur; isolated spots in hallways where certain students could gravitate outside of supervision; and poor bus-loading routines and areas that contribute to confusion and too many students congregated in one place. School staff established routines for moving through the school as well as entering and leaving and increased monitoring of the specific trouble spots.
- Scheduling issues including decreasing wait time and travel time between classrooms, lunch, recess, and so forth; clearly marking transition zones between a controlled area and common areas, letting students know where they were in the school and what was expected in each zone; and minimizing large groups of students, particularly cross-grades, in any contained part of the building or playground. Examples include the following: school staff established clear expectations for hallway behavior, and teachers stood outside their doors to monitor that movement; lunch and recess schedules were examined to ensure that students could move quickly from place to place by class or grade so as to avoid logjams in the hallways; and rules were also established for when students could go to lockers.

Behavioral expectations for all students were defined by teachers through a consensus-building process. Teachers first established expectations for the common areas or routines, lunch, arrival, and departure because the majority of problems occurred during these times. Following are some examples of the process that was put into place to inform and enforce behavioral expectations:

- Teachers broke the expectations into specific teachable behaviors, not just rules on a piece of poster board.

(Continued)

(Continued)

- Students were taught the expectations through a three-phase process: first they were highly supervised and given a lot of praise and corrective feedback for the first several weeks of school, then they were given periodic structured practice or review sessions, and finally, they had booster sessions as needed.
- Teachers agreed on common supervision strategies and a consistent approach. Teachers understood which behaviors warranted an office referral. They also learned a common set of interventions to problem behaviors that they were to implement in their classrooms or common areas.
- A one-to-one reading program was established along with a conflict resolution program.
- A family intervention specialist was brought in to develop a voluntary video-based program for families of students with the highest rate of discipline problems.
- Teams developed individualized BIPs for those students with the most serious or frequent behavioral problems.

The seven schools significantly reduced administrative disciplinary actions; increased academic achievement scores in reading, language arts, spelling, science, and social studies; and increased social competence and academic scores among students with the most challenging behaviors. In addition, teachers reported that they were highly satisfied with the process and outcomes.

BUILDING STRONG PARENT AND FAMILY CONNECTIONS

The final component of a good special education program is strong communication with parents and families. Parents and families have always been critical to achieving the goals of IDEA just as parents and families are important to schooling in general. In special education, the role of parents has been strengthened so that they may better participate in the decisions regarding their child. As stated in Section I, the IDEA gives parents and families certain rights to enable them to be full partners in developing their child's education.

Creating a collaborative relationship between parents of children with disabilities and educators is a major goal shared by parent advocates, administrators, and policymakers. A key factor in creating good partnerships with parents is understanding what constitutes *effective* parent involvement.

Box 2.10   Voices of Real Parents

"I really don't talk much at my son's IEP meetings because I am trying so hard not to cry. Even though he's 12, every time I go to the IEP meeting it just brings up again all the reality about his disability."

"I just wish the school would at least act like they liked my child and when my husband and I come in they would treat us more informally. They always act so formal and then we go into a room with all of these people sitting there who have been talking about our child . . . and us."

"We need respect. . . . We need to feel that our contribution is valued. We need to participate, not merely be involved. It is, after all, the parent who knew the child first and who knows the child best. Our relationship with our sons and daughters is personal and spans a lifetime."

Parents of Children With Disabilities

Principals are expected to work with all parents and their school community. It is particularly important that principals communicate, collaborate with, and involve parents in the education of their child with a disability in a positive way. Principals should expect that parents of children with disabilities be partners with the school and help resolve any issues that might arise, but parents are not to be solely responsible for resolving the problems. Principals may believe that they are doing every-thing possible to collaborate with the parents of children with disabilities and may honestly believe they are cooperating and communicating. However, from the parents' perspective, the interactions can be frustrat-ing. Often they do not feel that the school understands their unique con-cerns about their child's disability or that the school is making an effort to address the child's needs.

To be able to work effectively with parents of students with disabilities, a principal must understand and respect the perspective of those parents. Parents of children with disabilities, like all other parents, want a good education for their child, but they can also have additional anxieties about their child, including safety, peer acceptance, teasing or bullying, and fears that they are not learning or making enough progress. One parent shared the following: "We always need to be aware of new ideas or programs. We feel that if we miss something we will fail our child."

Parents experience intense emotions about their child's disability. For parents of a child who has a severe disability that might be diagnosed at birth or in the early years, these emotions can include anxieties about what the future holds. Parents whose children are diagnosed later after years of failure and problems in school are often frustrated and tired from the repeated calls from schools, conferences, and attempts to "fix" their child's problem. Many parents of children with disabilities feel guilty. Sometimes the emotional and physical weariness associated with parent-ing a child with a disability can immobilize parents. They may just give up, and then the school may see a parent who is not involved or doesn't care instead of a parent who needs support and validation. For other parents, the anxieties about their child lead them to be even more vigilant of the school and to question decisions made by the school.

Parents of children with disabilities can often feel powerless in the education process of their child. Despite the rights of parents of children with disabilities to be involved in all phases of their child's education program, the parents often do not feel competent to make critical deci-sions. They must rely on experts and professionals to explain to them what their child needs. This requires a great deal of trust, and often the professionals are strangers or merely acquaintances to the parents. Yet trust is the foundation of effective parent collaboration and involvement.

Involving Parents of Children With Disabilities in Schoolwide Activities

The IDEA makes it clear that parents of children with disabilities are to be involved in specific policymaking bodies. An important way to involve parents of children with disabilities is in the school improvement planning process. Asking these parents to review data concerning special education students and to be part of a process of developing school goals and activities, including those that may pertain specifically to children with disabilities, is important for many reasons. First, it engages these parents in the school community. Sometimes the parents of children with disabilities do not feel connected to a school. If this is not the home school of the child and the family is not part of the neighborhood, there can be a greater distance between the school and the parents. Second, it is important for all parents to see the big picture in terms of what the school as a whole is moving toward as well as how special education fits within the overall program. Many parents can develop tunnel vision when it comes to their child's needs. It is important for every parent to understand their child's needs within the context of the larger school. But often parents of children with disabilities feel that they have been shut out of decision making in schools. Make sure that when you do involve parents in school-wide plans that you are hearing the voices of all the parents, including parents of children with various disabilities.

Communicating With Parents

A good relationship with parents depends on open communication and access to the teacher, a counselor, a school psychologist, and/or the principal. Principals need to ensure that parents have opportunities to communicate about their child. Developing an open and trusting relationship with one person is a key to good parental cooperation and communication.

Real participation can occur only when you have informed parents. Don't be afraid of giving information to parents of children with disabilities. Open communication is part of building trust. Make certain that they have information about their rights is critical (school districts must provide information about parent's rights), but parents need other information or resources as well. Perhaps your special education director can provide some materials, or you can direct a parent to one of the many Web sites that have excellent information or to the local parent information training center. If there is something you don't know, say so and ask the parent for information.

Parents of children with disabilities often seek more in-depth information regarding school expectations. For example, parents may need more information about testing programs and how to interpret test scores or grades. They may also want other information to help them understand how well their child is progressing. For instance, simply telling a parent

The Web site http://www.nichcy.org is a particularly good resource for materials to help you inform and involve parents in your school.

that his or her child is below grade level in reading or writing is not enough. Parents frequently comment that they know their child is not doing grade-level work, but what they really want to know is whether the child is improving in reading or math. They want to know what they can expect by next year. They want to know if they need to do something different. Help parents understand which skills are posing problems and what is being done, and give concrete examples of improvement. Encourage all staff to use layperson language and make it a practice to do a language check in IEP or other meetings with the parents. Just pause and ask if anyone has any questions about a word or term that has been used.

In short, principals must assume leadership for ensuring parental involvement, including assessing the degree to which parents are participating in the education of their child and how satisfied they are with the opportunities for involvement. The goal for principals should be to create a partnership with parents, based on mutual respect and understanding. This will require open communication, trust, respect, and time on the part of staff and the building leader.

In Section III, I discuss the basic strategies necessary to create effective special education in schools as well as the evidence base for what works in current special education.

Creating Quality Special Education

The Context

Key Ideas for Section III

➢ High-quality special education programs must be built around instructional practices with a proven track record and backed by credible research.
➢ Principals need skills for making data-based decisions about students with disabilities and special education services.
➢ Quality special education requires flexibility and collaboration in a school.

ADOPT EVIDENCE-BASED PRACTICES

Among the new responsibilities of school leaders is ensuring that decisions to implement specific instructional models or curricular approaches are based on credible research. A principal must be able to help all staff in the school investigate the instructional practices they choose and select only those that have a proven record of success. Both the NCLB and IDEA refer to the need to use scientifically validated practices or evidence-based practices.

On a daily basis, principals are faced with a barrage of commercial advertisements touting everything from student fund-raising schemes to budget management software, reading curricula, professional development programs, and all types of technology. In addition, principals are often faced with opportunities to participate in model programs or to write grants for special programs. If you are a fan of the marketplace, you might welcome the availability of a wide variety of approaches and options in all aspects of the conduct of school business. However, as the number of education entrepreneurs has increased in recent years, so has the number of education snake oil dealers. The problem for school leaders is that sometimes it is very difficult to tell the difference. Box 3.1 contains an example.

Box 3.1   An Example of Principal Decision Making

Mr. Baker receives a call from Dr. Samson-White, the local representative of CogniTSoft Systems, a software and curriculum publisher that has been in business about eight years. He knows her because she used to teach fifth grade in his former school and has worked as an instructor for the local university. Dr. Samson-White tells Mr. Baker that her company has just released Reading for the World, an innovative reading and professional development program aimed at the middle school level. The program employs leading edge technology and a new multimedia approach to reading instruction for middle school. It includes a variety of Web-based, high interest activities for students and a series of colorful, culturally responsive classroom materials. When Dr. Samson-White tells him that the program is "linked to our state reading standards," Mr. Baker gets interested, because too many seventh-grade students in his school have not been proficient in reading for the past three years. He gets really excited when she informs him that CogniTSoft also is releasing the Reading for the World Professional Development Academy to accompany the student program. This package academy includes cyber-classes, in-person consultants, and a variety of attractive support materials geared toward novice teachers and mentors. Staff turnover has been a problem in Mr. Baker's school, and he recently initiated a support program for new teachers. The Reading for the World program seems like the perfect solution to his problems, and the program is competitively priced.

Should Mr. Baker buy the Reading for the World program? What criteria should he use to decide? Let's look at some of the questions he should ask:

- *Can he afford it?*—Probably. CogniTSoft no doubt has done extensive marketing research and is pricing the various components of the program at points that are consistent with the budgets of a majority of middle school reading programs.
- *Is it recommended by a trusted source?*—Yes. He knows Dr. Samson-White as a sincere professional who believes in the product she is selling.
- *Does it meet a need?*—Clearly. This program addresses two key areas of concern for Mr. Baker: middle school reading and new teacher development.
- *Does it have a solid reputation?*—It's a new program using new technology and a new approach to instruction. Mr. Baker doesn't have much to go on here, does he?

Box 3.2   "Bad" Education Ideas

Listed below are some instructional practices that were implemented in public schools in the not-too-distant past that we now know don't work:

- Early in the 20th century, seats and desks were bolted to the floor of classrooms. Then, in the 1960s and 1970s, school designers experimented with open designs in which classrooms were separated by moveable walls or even partitions. We now know that neither of these designs worked all that well.
- When we thought that learning disabilities were caused by deficits in sensory integration, many schools hired occupational and physical therapists to conduct sensory integration therapy. Students receiving this treatment were spun around on swings, walked on balance beams, and rolled around on therapy balls. We now know that sensory integration therapy doesn't have much effect on the academic performance of students with learning disabilities.

(Continued)

(Continued)

- The standard practice in reading classrooms has been, for years, ability-organized reading groups, where one student reads and the rest of the students in the group follow along and listen. We now know that students learn best when instruction actively engages them and they receive effective feedback. Passively following along does little to improve the performance in reading.

- When computers were first introduced into schools, they were perceived as specialized equipment that needed to be located in computer labs, and computer skills were taught in isolation, separate from the rest of curriculum. These computer labs often remained empty for large parts of the school day and so the computers went unused. As the price of computers has steadily dropped, and as we have learned more about how to integrate computers into teaching and learning, we now know that it is better to distribute computers throughout the school building and use them as part of a specific curriculum.

- Age- and grade-equivalent scores are reported by most major test publishers and continue to be used widely to describe student performance. However, age- and grade-equivalent scores are based on the false assumption that learning progresses in a linear fashion from year to year. We all know that children learn in fits and starts, with big gains in some years and small gains in others. These scores have been widely discredited by all major educational and psychological professional organizations.

- Organizing high schools into ability tracks was an accepted practice for most of the 20th century. We now know that ability tracking benefits only the students in the very top tracks and works to the disadvantage of virtually everyone else in the school.

All instructional practices are not created equal. The problem Mr. Baker faces is that it is not always immediately clear from simply observing a classroom or talking to a teacher whether an instructional practice is likely to succeed. Practices that seem like a great idea at the time later turn out to be instructional bombs, while other practices that may seem, at first glance, unlikely to help children learn, turn out to be highly effective. Some approaches and strategies work well for some students but not others, and some instructional practices work for some teachers but not others. An alarming number of instructional practices found in schools today don't actually work too well for anyone.

WHAT ARE EVIDENCE-BASED PRACTICES?

Building a high-quality program where all students are learning requires proven instructional practices. But just what are proven instructional practices? These are practices that have been subjected to scientific testing and found to be consistently effective. Proven instructional practices produce the kinds of effects they claim, across many applications.

Proven instructional practices have two key characteristics:

1. They have been validated by scientific studies.

2. They have been examined by the larger educational community.

The process of verifying and validating the effectiveness of an instructional practice requires conducting multiple carefully controlled studies. To understand how a particular program or intervention may be considered effective, a review of some research principles is in order.

There are two large categories of types of research: quantitative and qualitative. Quantitative research allows investigation of cause and effect relationships and is considered to be a higher standard of research validation. Quantitative methods of data are necessary to answer questions such as "How did this specific instructional method affect students?" Qualitative research is appropriate when a researcher is searching for broader patterns or is seeking to situate an educational practice in a larger societal or policy context. Qualitative research can be appropriate to answer questions such as "How did a school go about implementing a new curriculum and what barriers did it face?" Neither approach to research is right or wrong. In fact, both types of research are necessary to make good choices about programs. What is important is that the research should be conducted in accordance with accepted scientific and ethical standards established by the major research organizations in our profession, such as the American Educational Research Association and the American Psychological Association.

**Box 3.3   What's the Difference Between Qualitative
and Quantitative Research?**

Types of Questions

- Quantitative research generally involves very specific questions about relationships among larger groups or populations, for example, the reading achievement of first-grade students taught phonemic awareness or drop-out rates of Hispanic boys in high schools that have implemented high stakes testing.
- Qualitative research generally involves intense examination of a specific situation to address broad, nonspecific questions, for example, the leadership style of three middle school principals or the cooperative culture in two urban third-grade classrooms.

Objectivity

- Quantitative research generally involves objective data-collection strategies and statistical analysis. For example, a researcher might collect reading test scores from a group of first graders who had been taught phonemic awareness and from a comparable group who had not been taught phonemic awareness and then compare these scores using analysis of variance.
- Qualitative research generally employs subjective data-collection and analysis strategies. For example, a qualitative researcher might conduct a series of interviews with a small number of participants and then look for themes across those interviews.

Generalizability

- Quantitative studies attempt to control the influence of random events that are irrelevant to the central question being investigated. Therefore, quantitative researchers intend for the results of their studies to be applicable to all other situations that are similar to the one they have studied. For example, a quantitative researcher likely would expect that any findings about the reading achievement of the first graders in a particular study could be generalized to all first graders.

- Qualitative researchers make no claims of generalizability of their results beyond the specific situation they examine. For example, a qualitative researcher probably would not suggest that the leadership styles of the three particular middle school principals in a study would necessarily be similar to that of other middle school principals who were not in the study.

THE IMPORTANCE OF USING PUBLISHED RESEARCH

Scientific rigor also means that the results of research are reported and available for examination by the larger educational research community. Anecdotal reports of effectiveness do not constitute scientific scrutiny and neither do written reports or materials that have not been subject to outside review. Any practice that is called effective should be backed up with written descriptions of the supporting research that answers who, when, where, and what happened. Generally, this public reporting is accomplished through publication in credible research publications or sometimes through presentation of the results at research conferences.

In the not-too-distant past, educators relied primarily on scholarly journals to present findings of research. These journals contain articles written by experts or scholars in the field and are intended for other scholars and practitioners in the profession. The reason that many of these articles often are technical is that scientific rigor requires that research provide enough information to allow others to replicate the research. Articles published in scientific journals are reviewed by a board of knowledgeable scholars whose job it is to check the quality of the research. In contrast, articles in the popular press, such as magazines (paper or electronic), contain few, if any, references, often are written by journalists or laypersons who have little specialized knowledge of the topic, and are written for consumption by the general public. Many of the commercially available educational materials also do not contain any research or references to substantiate the product.

With the growth of the Internet, the sources of information about instructional practices have exploded. Reports of research about instructional practices are published routinely on the World Wide Web by government agencies, publicly funded research institutes, private foundations, professional organizations, and a wide variety of public and private special interest groups.

In the middle ground between scholarly journals and magazines are publications or Web sites devoted to the practical concerns of teaching or administering educational programs. Articles in practitioner journals tend to be more general than those in scholarly journals and written for a broader audience of practitioners in the profession who are not necessarily going to replicate a study. These publications can be useful for tracking trends or finding accounts of field-based applications of instructional practices. Regardless of the type of publication or medium you use, you should look for certain critical information to judge the quality of a specific practice.

Standards for Evaluating the Quality of Research

The What Works Clearinghouse was established in 2002 by the U.S. Department of Education's Institute of Education Sciences (IES) to provide educators, policymakers, researchers, and the public with a central and trusted source of scientific evidence of what works in education.

Evidence Standards established by the IES rate practices. Each study that has investigated a particular program or practice can receive one of three possible ratings:

- "Meets Evidence Standards" (for randomized controlled trials and regression discontinuity studies that provide the strongest evidence of causal validity).
- "Meets Evidence Standards with Reservations" (for quasi-experimental studies; randomized controlled trials that have problems with randomization, attrition, or disruption; and regression discontinuity designs that have problems with attrition or disruption).
- "Does Not Meet Evidence Standards" (for studies that do not provide strong evidence of causal validity).

The gold standard of educational research is experimental design, in which subjects are randomly assigned to treatment and control groups. Well-designed experimental studies allow clear, unambiguous decisions about the effectiveness of an intervention, because all of the irrelevant factors that could affect the outcome of the study have been eliminated. Box 3.4 provides an example of an experimental study.

Box 3.4   A Simple Education Experiment

Suppose Mr. Baker wants to find out if using a new writing software package improves students' ability to revise second drafts of their papers. He decides to run an experimental study. First he randomly assigns students to one of two treatments: the new software revising group and the paper-and-pencil revising group. Next, he makes certain that teachers provide exactly the same writing instruction to both groups. After the instruction is complete, both groups are given a writing and revising task to see which group does better on some objective measure of organization, cohesion, and mechanics. Mr. Baker then compares the results of evaluations of the students' writing to find out which group performed better. He repeats the experiment with several other groups to compare his results.

Because experimental designs always involve random assignment of subjects to treatment and control groups, careful manipulation of treatment and control conditions, and use of a common measure of outcomes, we have much more confidence in the results of experimental studies than we do in other designs. For this reason, experimental studies are commonly used in medical research, where the costs of making a wrong inference on the basis of a study can be very high.

Of course, educational researchers can't always randomly assign students to separate treatment groups. There may be logistic or ethical considerations, or the instructional practice being studied may not lend itself to manipulation in an experimental study. You couldn't randomly assign students to a poor-reading-instruction group or a no-math instruction group.

There are a variety of high-quality research designs that don't involve randomization. Indeed, most of the research that is done in education involves procedures that are not, strictly speaking, experimental. Other widely used and respected empirical research designs may involve surveys, interviews, observations, and case studies. In fact, there are so many designs used in educational research that it can be difficult to decide whether a particular instructional intervention has been validated scientifically. However, there are some key features that all high-quality research has in common:

- *Peer Review*—Organizations and individuals who are honestly concerned with increasing the knowledge base in our profession are not afraid to subject their work to the scrutiny of informed peers in the profession. This is where examination by the larger educational community takes place. It is important to know your sources. Is the journal or publication you rely on to inform you of new practices using outside reviewers who are independently judging the quality of the research?

- *Representative Samples*—Quantitative research is premised on the idea that the results obtained from a small sample can be generalized or applied to a larger population. Therefore, it is a rule of thumb that the more a sample in a study resembles the students in your school, the more applicable the results of the study are for your students. For example, if your school includes a high number of students who speak Spanish as their first language, you would want to make sure that the instructional approaches you adopt in your school have been researched with Spanish-speaking students. Similarly, you might want to be sure that research was conducted in real classrooms with real teachers and not just at a laboratory school or in a highly controlled setting.

- *Adequately Sized Samples*—In addition to the characteristics of the study sample, you also should be concerned with the size of the sample. There is no single hard-and-fast rule for determining an adequate sample size, but in general, more is better. Most research designs require samples of at least 25 subjects in each group being examined. The exceptions to this rule are qualitative and single-subject studies, which often involve only a few subjects. In the latter case, you would want to see the same results achieved over multiple trials with different students.

- *Reliable and Valid Measures*—Most educational studies involve some sort of measurement system. For example, students in two different reading treatments might be given a reading test at the beginning and end of the study. It is critical that the measures used to evaluate an instructional approach meet the same standards of technical adequacy as we require of other testing systems in schools. The measures must have high reliability and must yield valid decisions about the variable being examined. I discuss these important concepts in more detail later.

- *Replication*—This means there have been multiple research studies in different contexts to find out if the same results are obtained. Usually, replication involves a different set of participants and often involves systematic change of some aspect of the original study, while retaining its essential elements. You should be suspicious when an instructional practice has only been investigated by one researcher or a few of that researcher's associates or if different researchers report drastically different findings.

QUALITY OF EVIDENCE

While there are sources that provide information on these strategies or programs that are evidence-based, what do you do if you are interested in a program that has yet to be evaluated? There are two criteria you can use to evaluate the quality of the evidence regarding instructional practices: quantity of evidence and credibility of evidence. Figure 3.1 provides an example that illustrates these criteria.

The chart shown in Figure 3.1 is similar to the one the U.S. Government Accountability Office (GAO) eventually developed to display its evaluation scheme. The horizontal axis refers to the quality of the evidence that supports a practice, while the vertical axis refers to the quantity of information about the practice.

Some instructional practices are widely discussed in the professional literature and popular press, but they have not been validated in studies that employ the standards of quality I discussed earlier. These studies would be found in the area marked by the "1" in the figure. It is difficult to tell if these practices are really effective or are simply a passing fad getting an inordinate amount of media attention. Popular isn't the same as *effective.*

Other practices may have been researched in very-well-designed, high-quality studies, but only a few studies of the practice have been conducted. These practices may be effective, but much more replication is needed. Practices such as these would be found in the area marked by the "2" in the figure. New and emerging instructional practices that have not been validated in rigorous research and are not widely described in the literature would be found in the area marked by the "3" in the figure. Locally developed curricula and many classroom-based interventions would fall into this category. The most desirable combination of quality and quantity of evidence is

Two excellent sources of research-validated interventions for students with disabilities are as follows:

- The What Works Clearinghouse aims to promote informed education decision making through a set of easily accessible databases and user-friendly reports that provide education consumers with high-quality reviews of the effectiveness of replicable educational interventions (programs, products, practices, and policies) that intend to improve student outcomes (see http://ies.ed .gov/ncee/wwc/overview/).
- The NICHCY National Dissemination Center for Children with Disabilities Research-to-Practice database allows you to browse by topic, age and grade level, or even conduct a keyword search. The database, which is continually updated, evaluates various interventions, practices, and programs for students with disabilities and presents summaries of those that have substantial

Figure 3.1   Quality of Studies and Credibility of Information

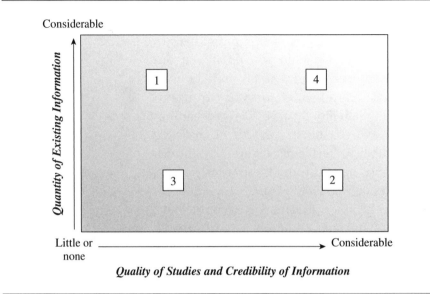

Quality of Studies and Credibility of Information

SOURCE: Adapted from Hunt (1996).

represented by the area marked with a "4" in the figure. These are interventions that have been validated by rigorous research employing the standards discussed earlier and have been widely described in the research literature. These are the interventions you generally will want to adopt in your school.

DATA-BASED DECISION MAKING

Throughout this book, I have emphasized that the key to ensuring the success of all children in your school is good problem solving. There are no one-size-fits-all answers. What works for one student or age group may not be right for another and what works in someone else's school may not be successful in yours. Principals need effective decision tools to determine what works and what doesn't. In Section II, I presented decision frameworks for aligning IEPs with standards, for selecting accommodations and modifications, and for designing positive behavioral supports. Earlier in this section, I discussed the importance of selecting scientifically proven instructional approaches and for understanding the science underlying those approaches. However, even when you use systematic decision frameworks and select scientifically sound interventions, you still need to collect data to evaluate your decisions.

Box 3.5   The Data-Driven Compact Car

In the late 1950s, a number of small European cars, such as Volkswagens, Saabs, Volvos, and Renaults, were beginning to make a dent in the U.S. automobile market. They were inexpensive, fun to drive, and relatively trouble free. U.S. car manufacturers decided they needed to offer their own compact cars. In 1960, after extensive market research and some reverse engineering, Chevrolet introduced the Corvair to compete primarily with the Volkswagen Beetle. Like the Beetle, it had a rear, air-cooled engine, fully independent suspension, and a unitized body. These were all firsts for an American car manufacturer. In 1961, Chevrolet introduced a Corvair station wagon, a van, and a pickup truck, mirroring the offerings of Volkswagen at the time. Chevrolet continued manufacturing Corvairs until the 1968–1969 model year. Today, most people assume that Ralph Nader's book (1965), *Unsafe at Any Speed*, detailing problems with the rear suspension on the early models, is what killed the Corvair. In fact, the suspension problems described in Nader's book were corrected by the 1964 model year and a 1972 report by the National Highway Safety Administration noted that the Corvair was as safe as most other cars on the road at the time. Chevrolet stopped making the Corvair because its own research department collected data that indicated consumers wanted bigger muscle cars like the Camaro and Corvette. Gasoline was cheap and growing baby-boomer families needed more room.

Data-based decision making brought the Corvair into existence and data resulted in its demise.

Data and information are powerful tools for school leaders who aim to create high-quality special education programs. School leaders must understand and use a variety of information sources and know how to collect and analyze data. Data-based decision making is central to a process of continuous improvement, and it is absolutely necessary for the creation of high-quality special education programs.

As is the case with many tools, it takes skill and practice to use data effectively in making decisions. Being able to collect and analyze data isn't enough. Even the most experienced administrator can succumb to the perils of poor judgment using data for the wrong reason or going beyond one's data to make judgments that are not valid. To be an effective school leader you also need to be an effective decision maker and know how to avoid common errors of decision. In this section, I'll provide strategies to help you master data-based decision making.

Converting Data to Information

Data usually mean the results of measurements or observations, such as assessment scores; census, enrollment, or attendance rates; results of parent surveys; and a wide range of demographic data. Schools are data-rich environments. But decision makers must convert data into useful *information.* Data become information when they improve the knowledge of the people using the data so they are better able to make a decision. Principals need to know which data are important and which are not useful to their school improvement efforts.

Box 3.6   An Example of Data-Based Decision Making

Ms. Cabrera is the principal of Horizons Middle School. Six years ago she led the faculty in her school in developing a curriculum renewal initiative to better align the math and reading programs with state standards and assessments. The initiative included study groups in which small groups of teachers read and discussed various approaches to reading and math instructional research, thematic curriculum days, and team-building workshops for grade-level teams to improve planning and communication. Many of the teachers reported that they thought these processes were successful, and the study groups are now a part of the ongoing work of the school. For the past four years, reading scores on the seventh-grade statewide reading assessment have improved, with about 5% more students meeting standards each year. However, math scores have not improved as dramatically. This past year, 20% of the seventh graders who took the test were at advanced or proficient levels, but over the past three years, about 8% fewer students have met the basic math standard. Ms. Cabrera has scheduled a half-day meeting with her faculty to discuss assessment scores and the curriculum renewal process.

Ms. Cabrera and the faculty at Horizons Middle School have some difficult decisions to make, and the research about decision making suggests that they will probably attend to the wrong variables or misinterpret the information they have available to them.

What errors of judgment are Ms. Cabrera and her teachers on the verge of making? If you were planning the agenda for the Horizons Middle School meeting, what topics and activities would you include? Do you know how to avoid some common errors of judgment and decision making that the team is at risk of committing? After you read this section, return to this scenario and see if your advice to Ms. Cabrera and her team has changed.

To be useful for decision making, data must be as current as possible. This means the interval between when data are collected, analyzed, and evaluated must be as short as possible. Data-based decision making should be a continuous process in which principals and school improvement teams identify the goals and desired outcomes they wish to achieve, clarify the decisions associated with those outcomes, and then collect, interpret, and use data to make decisions. This process is illustrated in Figure 3.2.

Let's look at each of the steps in this process.

Figure 3.2   Continuous Data-Based Decision Making

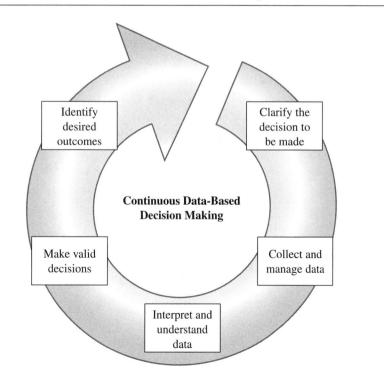

Identify Desired Outcomes

Decision making is always focused on a desired outcome. In schools, the outcomes with which educators usually are concerned pertain to student learning. However, other important data can include attendance or suspensions or other disciplinary actions. Student performance is affected by a wide variety of school-level inputs, such as teacher expertise, curriculum materials, scheduling, use of paraprofessionals, and school climate. Think about Ms. Cabrera and the faculty at Horizons Middle School. What outcomes might they want to achieve? No doubt they want to increase the number of students who meet standards on the seventh-grade math assessment. But how should they do it? Should they work to improve teacher skills? Should they adjust the schedule to allocate more time to math? Should they deploy paraprofessionals differently to provide more specialized instruction for the students with greatest needs? Do they need to revamp the math curriculum? Frequently, when school staff are confronted with a problem such as improving student achievement, they "throw everything" at the problem. That is, they want to try everything.

As a rule, the process of identifying desired outcomes (student achievement) should focus on variables over which the decision makers have the most direct control, rather than those over which they have relatively little impact. Principals can have direct control over how they allocate time and deploy teachers or other resources. Teachers can choose instructional strategies, design activities and lessons, and organize and manage classrooms. Principals and teachers have little or no control over things such as demographics, student mobility, legislated mandates concerning curricula and assessments, and budget allocations; they have limited control over teacher quality and parental support.

Principals should focus on information that most directly relates to the teaching and learning process. They should always consider credible evidence of student achievement first and then consider evidence related to implementing a procedure in the classroom and the classroom-level effects of their decisions. To set clear priorities, start at the student and classroom level and move outward. This proximal to distal decision-making process is illustrated in Figure 3.3.

Think about the goal of increasing the number of students who meet proficiency on the math assessment. There is a variety of decisions a principal could make to try to accomplish this goal. For example, increasing the amount of time allocated to math instruction in the morning is a variable over which a principal probably has direct control and that would have direct impact on students. This decision would be

Figure 3.3   A Decision-Making Framework

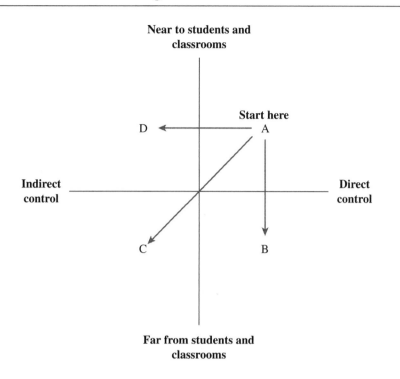

located in the quadrant marked A in Figure 3.3. A decision that also might have a direct impact on students is to increase the amount of time spent on math homework. Of course, principals and teachers have less control over how and whether homework gets done. This decision would be located in quadrant D. A decision in the B quadrant might be to provide incentives for teachers to take math classes. The benefits of this decision for students likely would be less direct, depending on which math classes teachers take and the extent to which this decision increased math knowledge used in the school. A decision in the C quadrant might be to improve community attitudes about math learning. A principal would likely have relatively little impact over community attitudes about math, and it is not likely that this change would make much difference on student test scores.

The optimum distribution of decisions in the four quadrants in Figure 3.3 will vary from school to school. But, if you find that your school has difficulty meeting its goals, you should examine your priorities. If you find that much of your attention is focused on variables in the C quadrant, look for ways to move your decision making toward A.

Clarify the Decision to Be Made

Once the desired outcomes for the decision process have been identified, you need to ask questions regarding the process:

1. *Is this a decision that involves data and information?* Sometimes the decisions over which we agonize most are not those that can be answered with data. For example, despite research that shows that adolescent brain development makes it difficult for middle and high school students to do school work early in the morning, the school day in many high schools starts as early as 7:00 A.M. to accommodate bus schedules, not student development.

2. *What information do we need to make this decision?* Make sure the data you want to collect and the decision you are making match your desired outcome. For example, if you are evaluating schoolwide, classroom-based interventions, you need to make sure you focus on data collected at the classroom level, such as weekly curriculum-based measures, homework assignments, and time allocated to instruction. Data from the annual assessments probably will not be sufficient.

3. *Who is going to make the decision?* Be sure you are realistic about who ultimately has responsibility for the decision you want to make. Is it a decision that can be made at the classroom or grade level or does it involve the entire school or maybe central office? Don't ask your teachers to invest time and energy on a decision that ultimately will be made by someone else, including yourself. On the other hand, if the success of an initiative is going to depend on the buy-in of teachers and staff, don't exclude them from the decision-making process. Their participation, or lack of it, is in itself a decision.

4. *What kind of decision are we making?* There are three kinds of information-based questions that school leaders typically need to answer (Husen & Postlethwaite, 1994).

   a. *What happened?* Questions are used to describe or evaluate specific programs or interventions. The data used to make these kinds of decisions are linked directly to a specific action being evaluated and generally will be collected in a particular classroom or school, rather than districtwide. For example, a high school principal might be interested in the effects of a schedule change on absenteeism among the current class of 10th-grade students, or a special education director might be interested in finding out if there are fewer new referrals in a particular middle school after a new schoolwide behavior management plan is implemented.

b. *Why did it happen?* Questions pertain to cause and effect relationships that may occur throughout an entire school or in schools across the district. For example, a curriculum coordinator may want to know why a reading program is more successful when implemented in second-grade classrooms than it is in third-grade classrooms, or the personnel director may want to find out why there have been more requests for transfers among teachers in one middle school than in another one across town with similar demographics. The data needed to make these decisions generally must be collected from larger groups and often involve more than one measure.

c. *Is there a trend?* Decisions involve analysis of data accumulated over time to identify or clarify trends. Trend questions require data that have been collected and organized the same way for the entire time period being analyzed and generally involve data collected at the building or district level. It is important to remember that trend analysis does not necessarily answer cause-and-effect questions. For example, there may be a variety of reasons why the math scores of seventh graders in a district have declined for the past five years. Math scores could be affected by curriculum, scheduling, the nature of the assessment system, or changes in demographics.

Collect and Manage Your Data

Data are collected and used for different purposes at different levels of the educational system. Continuous data-based decision making implies matching the data collected with the decisions being made. The most valid decisions are those that are based on information that is directly related to the decision. But administrators need to be sure that they are making the correct inferences about the data.

Direct measures of student performance require lower levels of inference. That is, student achievement or behavior is measured directly and within a reasonable time following intervention. The further removed the data are from the decision, the more susceptible the decision is to error. For example, scores from the statewide reading assessment may be useful for evaluating the effects of a curriculum your district is using, but they wouldn't be sufficient for making referrals to special education or changing particular instruction or curricular materials. Low scores on the assessment might support the conclusion that the curriculum didn't work, but these same low scores would not necessarily support the conclusion that a student needs to be referred to special education because he or she has a disability.

Different assessments have different sensitivities to change. The smaller the changes that are expected, the more sensitive assessment tools need to be. For example, most statewide assessments are intended to measure big changes at the school or district level over a year's time, not small weekly or monthly changes at the student or classroom level. In fact, statewide assessments are rarely if ever useful for the day-to-day decisions facing most school administrators. In part, that is because these assessments only "sample" the broad domain of knowledge and skills in a particular area. To adjust instruction, you need more data on performance on a large sample of the skills, concepts, and constructs.

To measure the effects of classroom-level interventions, teachers need to use classroom-based measures, administered weekly or monthly. To measure the effects of grade-level interventions, schools need to implement grade-level measures administered monthly or quarterly. Examples of classroom or grade-level measures may include locally developed curriculum-based assessments, systematic assessment of student work, teacher ratings, and observations or periodic surveys. Table 3.1 shows some examples of data collection strategies and the frequency with which they are implemented.

Data collection systems need to be efficient and tailored to the specific contexts of a school and district. The more that data collection is integrated into the day-to-day work of the school, the more efficient the process becomes. Also, a school with a higher population of non-English-speaking students may need to develop a variety of curriculum-based measures of math learning reflecting the languages spoken in the school. An English language, standards-based measure may miss improvements in math achievement actually being made in the school. However, curriculum-based measures cannot simply assess lower level skills. Therefore, teachers may need professional development in how to create good curriculum-based assessments as well as other strategies for assessing a students' progress in the curriculum.

Data collection systems must also meet minimum standards for technical soundness. *Reliability* is considered the minimally essential standard for determining data quality. Often, reliability is interpreted as relating to the stability or consistency of a test or assessment procedure. We might say a test is reliable if it yields the same kind of results time after time. However, it is probably more appropriate to think in terms of the idea that underlies reliability: random error. Random error is the static or noise a data system contains that may decrease the validity of the inferences you make. The term *reliable* really means free from random error.

Random error is a fact of life: All data systems contain random error. The more random error a measure contains (i.e., is influenced by factors that are irrelevant to what is being measured), the less reliable it is. Think about the sources of random error in the following examples.

A seventh-grade teacher is administering an end-of-the-unit science test in her fourth-period science class. On the morning of the test, the annual candy bar sale fund-raising campaign is launched at an all-school assembly. Does low performance on the test reflect students' science learning or the distraction of the assembly and sales campaign?

A school district has targeted written expression as a priority area for improvement among elementary schools. There have been a number of teacher professional-development training academies, and several high-profile consultants have conducted workshops. The writing section of the statewide test is scored by panels of teachers who are paid to attend a week-long working retreat at a lakeside resort complex. Last year, a new contractor was hired to manage this scoring retreat, and the training and scoring protocols used by the previous contractor were changed. Scores on the writing section for fourth graders were higher in 37% of the elementary schools in the district this year.

Because all data systems contain some amount of random error, no assessment task is completely reliable. Reliability is like happiness: it's always nice to have some, and the more you have, the better off you'll be. The prudent approach is to take as many steps as possible to ensure reliability during the planning, data collection, and analysis processes.

Table 3.1   Schedule for Progress Monitoring

Frequency	Procedure	Purpose
Once a year	State mandated, criteria-referenced achievement tests	Evaluate school effectiveness at teaching curriculum standards and benchmarks. Compare students and student subgroups within and across schools.
Three to four times a year	Locally developed (district- and school-developed) assessments linked to curriculum standards and benchmarks; use scoring rubrics and monitor individual student progress	Evaluate student progress in the curriculum frameworks
Once a month or once a week	Curriculum-based measures of larger subcomponent skills such as written expression and math problem solving; use scoring procedures and decision rules of basic skills such as oral reading fluency, math computation, or vocabulary; use objective scoring procedures and decision rules	Monitor progress in skills that are subcomponents of larger curriculum outcomes objectives; acquisition of basic skills associated with performance in larger domains

SOURCE: Adapted from Nolet and McLaughlin (2005).

Interpret and Understand Data

The best data system in the world is going to be useless if the decision makers using it don't understand how to interpret the results. More important, data-based decision making should involve all of the stakeholders in a school: teachers, administrators, paraprofessionals, parents, students, and community members. Therefore, principals have roles to play relative to data: First, they must know how to make sense of data, and then they must make sure staff understand the data they are to interpret. Here are some simple strategies for using data that can improve understanding.

Provide Clear Explanations—The data underlying most decisions in schools are relatively simple. They usually consist of scores that can be interpreted with some measure of central tendency (mean, median, mode), some measure of dispersion (range, standard deviation), or in terms of a ratio such as percentages. But even these common measures can cause confusion. Most teachers and many principals have had no more than one measurement course during their professional preparation. Most parents have had much less than that. Don't assume terms that are used widely in schools to talk about assessments are necessarily widely understood. If you want the teachers and parents to participate in the data-based decision-making process, they need clear explanations and definitions of the data. A strategy that some school leaders have found effective is to provide a one-page glossary of measurement terms whenever data are being reported.

Use Off-the-Shelf Data Management Tools—The more specialized data systems become, the more dependent administrators become on experts. Instead, look for ways to make every member of the school an expert in data utilization so that they can incorporate a data-based decision-making approach into their day-to-day work. Choose data tools that are widely available and can be used readily by teachers, paraprofessionals, and parents. Spreadsheet programs that are readily available can handle most data storage and analysis tasks at the school level. There are three arguments for using generic data tools. First, they tend to be less expensive than specialized data systems to acquire and to maintain. Second, technical and educational supports are widely available at low cost for most off-the-shelf systems. Third, because generic tools are widely available, many members of a faculty as well as parents may already know how to use them.

Keep It Simple and Flexible—Remember, the whole point of using data is to improve decision making. When data systems are unnecessarily complicated or specialized, it becomes more difficult to keep them updated, to extract useful information, or to see clear patterns, trends, and relationships. In general, build data systems that can be updated easily and often and that can serve multiple decisions. Optimally, one should collect data at the lowest level of aggregation possible. Usually, this means at the level of individual students. These data can always be aggregated up to the school level. Remember, start decision making at the student and classroom level and then move outward. The more data are combined across students, classrooms, and schools, the more information is lost. Let the computer do the work of computing aggregate data when needed.

Use Visual Displays—To understand data, a picture really is worth a thousand words. Whenever possible, present data using graphs and charts. Again, most off-the-shelf spreadsheet and word processing programs will have all the graphic tools needed. Never report data in only one format. If data are reported in text, also include a graphic. If data are reported in a table, try to find a way to also show it graphically. Use pie charts to show proportional data and bar charts to show central tendencies. Box plots can be used to show percentile ranks and dispersion as well as change over time. Tufte (1997, 2001) recommends using visual displays of data for two tasks that are particularly important for data-based decision making: showing change and showing comparisons. Some examples of visual displays that accomplish these tasks are shown in Figures 3.4 to 3.8.

Box plots, such as the one in Figure 3.4, are useful for communicating a great deal of information in a simple graphic. With raw scores provided on the vertical axis, the box itself shows the range of scores between the

Figure 3.4   Third-Grade Spring Oral Reading Fluency Scores

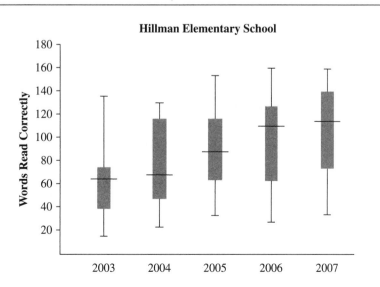

25th and 75th percentiles. The "whiskers" show the location of the 10th and 90th percentiles. The horizontal line within the box shows the median.

Time series data, such as those displayed in Figure 3.5, are useful for showing the progress of individual students. This graph shows the progress over 21 weeks for an individual student on a curriculum-based reading measure.

Figure 3.5   Use Individual Referenced Data to Show Change Over Time

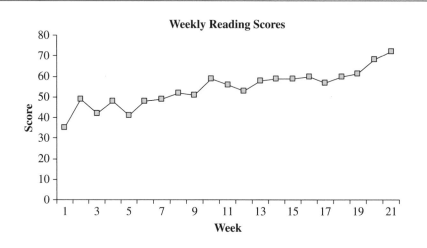

SOURCE: Taken from Hunt, E. S. (1996). *A Guide to the International Interpretation of U.S. Education Program Data: CIP, IPEDS, CCD, and ISCED.* U.S. Dept. of Education, Office of Educational Research and Improvement, Center for National Education Statistics, Office of Research, Washington, D.C.

Time series data also can show both change and comparison for groups. Figure 3.6 shows drop-out rates for three groups of students attending Stanton High School for the past 12 years. This graph indicates that after a steady decline in the late 1990s, drop-out rates for all three groups have gradually increased in the past seven years, with Hispanic students consistently dropping out at a higher rate than either White or African American students.

By organizing graphic displays of data into small multiples (Tufte, 2001), it is possible to compare the progress of a group of students or groups. Figure 3.7 shows the 21-week progress for six students who receive special education services for reading. Based on these data, is this special education program effective in improving reading?

Other types of graphic displays also can be presented in small multiples. Figure 3.8 shows the performance of fifth-grade students across the district, disaggregated by campus. At a glance, one can see which schools are in most need of assistance to increase test scores.

Figure 3.6 Drop-Out Rates at Stanton High School, 1996–2008

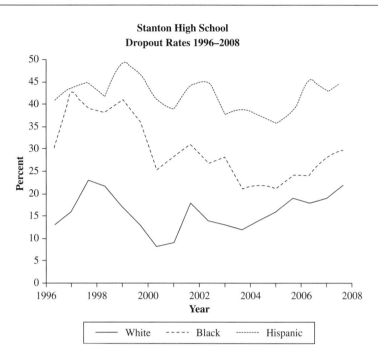

Make Valid Decisions

The quality of any decision depends directly on the quality of the information that is used to make the decision. The standard we use to judge the quality of a decision is validity. While validity often is treated as an attribute inherent to tests, it is more accurate to refer to the validity of decisions based on some data or information.

Validity involves both data and logical reasoning. No matter how well intentioned, decisions that are based on bad data cannot be valid. Similarly, no matter how good the data are, they can still be used for bad decisions. For example, in many schools, when high stakes testing is implemented and low scores are obtained, the initial response of administrators is to focus on superficial variables, such as teaching students how to take assessments, practicing items from old tests, or even providing orange juice and doughnuts to students to increase their energy before a test. These strategies may build up scores the first time but will not sustain progress. Instead the focus should be placed on the systematic issues of curriculum and its alignment with what is being assessed and what teachers are teaching. The good data obtained from the assessment system are used to make bad decisions to fiddle around the edges rather than to tackle the substantial and more difficult work associated with improving student learning.

Figure 3.7   Small Multiples Show 21 Weeks of Data for Six Students

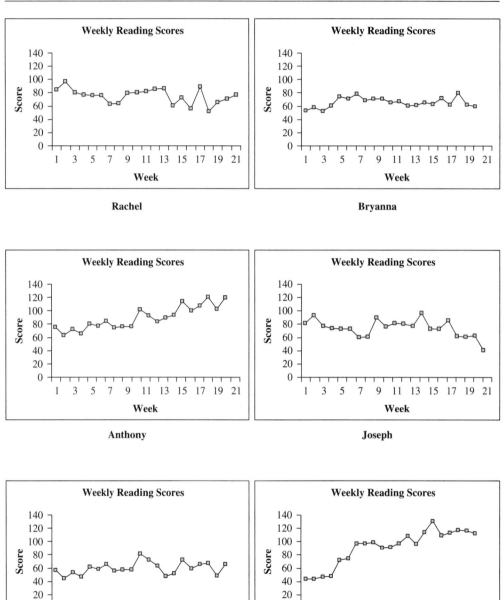

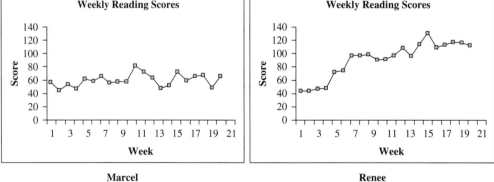

Weekly reading fluency scores for fourth grade
students with IEP goals in reading.

Figure 3.8   2006 Assessment Results for All District Fifth Grades

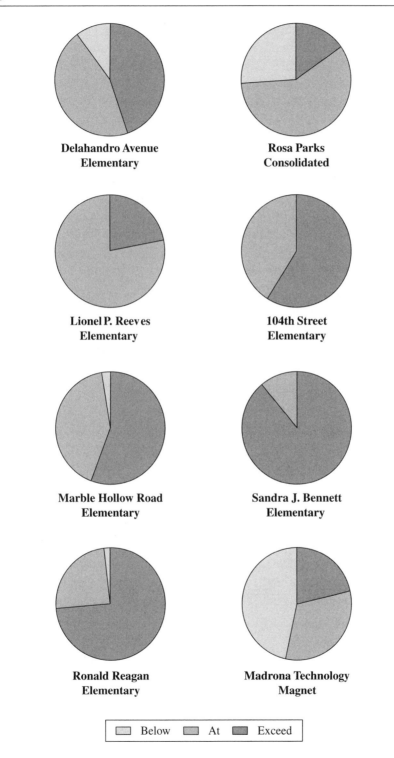

Validity is really more a relative than an absolute term: Some inferences or interpretation of information are more or less valid than others, depending on the strength of the evidence supporting them. A decision is valid when it's based on evidence in the form of real data. Often it is a good idea to explicitly list the evidence that contributes to the validity of a decision. This makes it easier to involve all stakeholders in the decision process and to understand the reasoning used to arrive at a decision. Decisions based on meager evidence are the ones that ultimately cause the most difficulty and are the least valid. That is why the randomized controlled studies are considered to be the "gold standard" for research. They can provide the strongest case for cause and effect. But many decisions that a principal must make do not lend themselves to this kind of rigorous study.

Researchers have used the term *triangulation to* refer to the use of multiple methods of data collection from a variety of sources to obtain a more complete picture on which to base inferences or decisions. The term suggests that it is possible to triangulate on the true state of affairs by obtaining multiple compass readings. Ideally, principals should collect two forms of evidence: data that confirm the decision or course of action they plan to take and data that fail to confirm an opposing view or alternate decision. The idea is that if a decision is the right one, things that should go together do go together, and things that shouldn't go together don't.

Avoid Errors of Judgment

Decision making is the process of choosing a course of action from among a set of alternatives. In an ideal world, we would be able to weigh the options objectively and arrive at a single best decision. Unfortunately, decisions pertaining to public schools often involve some degree of uncertainty, and of course, usually the sources of uncertainty are far beyond our control. For example, changes in the economy can have a drastic effect on variables such as local school demographics, the availability of highly qualified teachers, and community support for bond issues. Similarly, changes in the political makeup of a state legislature or even local school board can have immediate impacts on a wide range of policies and priorities.

School leaders often need to make decisions on the basis of some information that they can neither look up nor calculate. For example, it might be necessary to estimate the size of next fall's kindergarten class, the performance of the seventh-grade class on the statewide assessment to be administered next spring, or the time needed to complete a curriculum revision project.

In the absence of a crystal ball, it is useful to have heuristics, or rules of thumb for decision making under uncertainty. However, heuristics are, by definition, imperfect rules, so it is important to know how much confidence to place in them to avoid making errors of judgment.

The Availability Heuristic—When asked to judge the frequency or likelihood of an event, people tend to be influenced by how available that event is in their immediate environment. This error may cause them to make inaccurate judgments about incidence or cause-and-effect relationships. For example, a principal who works in a school with a high percentage of native English speakers may underestimate the number of non-English speakers in the district. Similarly, a sixth-grade teacher whose class, by chance, contains many students with poor reading skills may lament the inadequacy of the reading instruction of the lower grade teachers.

The Representativeness Heuristic—Often, it is necessary to judge whether a particular event is an example or representative of some larger category of events or situations. The mistake people often commit is to make this decision on the basis of superficial or extraneous characteristics. Here are some examples:

- A principal is interviewing a newly enrolled fourth-grade student and her mother. The mother speaks English with a heavy Spanish accent, so the principal assumes that the student will need English language instruction.
- A teacher sees that a third-grade boy has poor handwriting and gets low marks on his spelling tests. She assigns the student to the low-middle reading group because she believes his handwriting and spelling make this student similar to students with poor reading skills.
- A ninth-grade social studies teacher resists making accommodations for a student with a learning disability because he thinks the student just seems like a typical disorganized adolescent who needs to learn how to take more responsibility.

The *availability* and *representativeness* heuristics can be helpful when used in the presence of data. For example, if a principal wants to know how likely it is that the fifth graders at her school will reach proficiency on the statewide assessment, she might consider the degree to which they represent the group of previous fifth graders who met the standard on the test. To make that judgment, she would want to look at meaningful data pertaining to other assessments, curriculum alignment, and instructional variables in the classroom.

Unfortunately, once a decision has been made, people often resist adjusting that decision, even when additional data are present. Research has shown that decision makers tend to make only minor adjustments to an initial best guess, regardless of how inaccurate is their original estimate.

Of course, being conservative in adjusting initial decisions can serve us well. For example, a well-established method or belief should only be rejected when there is sufficient evidence that it isn't working. Yet, it seems that when an individual makes a judgment, his or her first estimate anchors the decision so firmly that the individual tends to make adjustments to the decision only grudgingly and tends to challenge the reliability or relevance of new information that supports a different decision. This phenomenon, known as *cognitive anchoring*, may be the single most difficult challenge to implementing a data-based decision-making system.

There is no foolproof way to avoid decision errors, but basing decisions on reliable data can help. By encouraging all members of a school to follow a data-based decision-making process, principals can prevent some errors of judgment.

CREATING SHARED RESPONSIBILITY FOR STUDENTS WITH DISABILITIES

Effective school leaders know that they can promote the success of all students by creating and sustaining a school culture that is conducive to student learning and professional growth and respect. Creating a climate that supports teachers while promoting continuous improvement is critical to effective special education. As special education is in the midst of some significant changes, in terms of both policies and school-level practices, today's school administrators must help teachers reshape beliefs and attitudes toward students with disabilities as they implement a shared vision of high expectations for all students.

Box 3.7   Collective Responsibility

Valerie Lee, an educational researcher at the University of Michigan, along with her colleagues, has studied the impact of school culture and teacher expectations on student achievement. Her research points to the importance of having teachers assume personal responsibility for student achievement as well as for all faculty in a school to share what she calls "collective responsibility" for the achievement of all children. This research has demonstrated that in schools with high levels of collective responsibility where there are consistent and high expectations among faculty, students learn more in all subjects. Lee has devised a collective responsibility scale that can measure the degree to which a school's faculty shares a common commitment to student achievement (see, e.g., Lee & Loeb, 2000).

As I noted at the beginning of this book, principals in the past often delegated responsibility for special education to a lead special education teacher. Distributing leadership for day-to-day special education decisions can be a perfectly good idea as long as the principal is fully accountable for the students who receive special education services and aware of what constitutes effective special education practice. Every decision a principal makes that directly impacts teaching and learning must be evaluated in terms of the evidence supporting effectiveness with all students, including those with disabilities. Principals must make certain that school improvement plans address the unique needs of students with disabilities and their families. This means that all data should be disaggregated, including parent satisfaction or climate surveys and other nonachievement data. In short, principals must create a unified staff with shared goals.

A number of studies have shown that teacher expectations about their students and their willingness to assume responsibility for the outcomes of their teaching have important consequences for learners. Research on school organization has pointed to the importance of fostering shared norms and values among teachers that emphasize academic growth and personal development for all students. For students who receive special education, general educators often assume that they can't teach the student who has an IEP and that the student's low achievement or behavioral problems are "part of the disability" and expected. General education teachers often do not feel responsible for teaching students with disabilities who may require specialized instruction or many modifications because they feel that they don't have the knowledge. Likewise, special educators can convey negative expectations to these students by trying to protect them from failure through reducing demands and "dumbing down" curriculum, as well as providing excessive support and assistance.

How all teachers interact with students shapes a school culture and influences students' beliefs about their own abilities. Imagine how a student feels who each day must face classrooms where he or she not only struggles to make sense of the instruction but also perceives that the teachers do not believe that he or she can succeed. Over time these negative classroom and school cultures alienate and anger some students; some may act out, while others withdraw. Many of these students disengage entirely from school and eventually stop coming altogether.

COLLABORATION BETWEEN GENERAL AND SPECIAL EDUCATORS

Special and general education collaboration is a required ingredient of special education. Collaboration is part of effective prereferral classroom interventions, RtI, positive behavior and support strategies that reduce discipline problems, and instructional practices that ensure that *all* students receive access to the same curriculum. Collaboration is a central feature in many of the new IDEA provisions, because collaboration can result in better outcomes for students with disabilities.

One example of the importance of general and special education collaboration can be found in several national projects funded by the Office of Special Education Programs to identify and study schools that were "Beacons of Excellence" for all students. A total of 10 "Beacons" schools, including elementary, middle, and high schools, were identified across the country that were obtaining exemplary results for both special and general education students. These were intensively studied over four years to identify key indicators of success. Across all sites, a common set of characteristics was identified. The most prominent feature of these schools was a strong collaborative culture that included all staff and administrators.

There are several different ways that special and general education teachers can collaborate within schools and classrooms. Coteaching and collaborative consultation are probably the most common. An important feature of both of these approaches is the emphasis on equality between teachers in terms of responsibilities and roles and shared problem solving and planning.

Collaborative Consultation

Collaborative consultation can take several forms but differs from the *expert-novice* or direct expert consultation approach that is often seen in education. In almost all situations, teachers often find the expert model of consultation to be ineffective. Often the solutions to problems presented by individual students require some change in what a teacher is doing, A teacher may have to change some aspect of his or her instruction or classroom organization or may have to provide more intensive instruction. Directing someone to teach differently is not effective. Working with someone collaboratively to assess educational problems, design interventions, and then supporting them as they try out their solutions results in change. The key to successful collaborative consultation is to strike the right balance between providing new information or skills and engaging in mutual problem solving that allows the individual teacher to choose and adapt solutions. However, in some cases a specialist may be required to diagnose a particular condition and propose a specific treatment or provide information about new instructional intervention.

Box 3.8   Lessons From "Beacons of Excellence" Schools

Key Indicators of a Collaborative School

- Special education is not a place or a parallel program. Students with disabilities and special education teachers are flexibly integrated into classrooms and the school.
- There are clearly articulated and shared expectations that every child in the school can achieve at higher levels and that achievement is valued. Teachers also believe that they can improve every student's performance.
- There is one curriculum aligned with standards and all staff understand the curricular goals.
- Every student's IEP is guided by the state curriculum standards and performance expectations.
- Special and general education teachers and paraprofessionals work together to design accommodations and modifications and provide individualized instruction to help students with disabilities access the general curriculum.
- General and special education teachers have the time, support, and flexibility needed to collaborate in a variety of ways. In general, special educators provide specific accommodations and specialized instructional strategies, and the general education teacher guides instruction in subject matter content.
- Related services, particularly speech and language therapists, provide therapy that is both integrated into and supports the curriculum and meets individual student needs.
- Open and ongoing communication between teachers and parents is expected and supported by the principal.

A number of collaborative consultation models have been successfully implemented in schools to assist teachers with students who are experiencing academic or behavioral problems. Some of these are the problem-solving RtI models discussed in Section I. Often these approaches have been used to prevent inappropriate referrals to special education. These consultation teams have many names, such as teacher assistance team, prereferral intervention team, and instructional consultation team. They almost always involve teachers, school psychologists, counselors, and other specialists as needed.

The effectiveness of these consultation models can vary greatly across schools. Much depends on how well the model is implemented. Effectiveness depends on the buy-in of individual teachers and their willingness to trust the team, problem solve with the team, and make a sincere and sustained effort to implement specific interventions. Some of the major reasons that collaborative consultation teams fail to resolve individual student problems are lack of specificity regarding the student's problem, lack of sufficient expertise among team members with respect to providing differentiated instructional strategies and curriculum adaptations, lack of data on the success of the model, and lack of follow-through on the part of the referring teacher.

Consultation teams must have the collective expertise to carefully isolate and document the student's learning or behavior problem that has prompted a teacher to seek help from the team. This means listening to the teacher as well as collecting data on the student's actual behavior or performance. Both formal and informal assessments of student skill levels or other behaviors are required as discussed earlier in this section.

A team must also be able to generate workable solutions. This requires mutual problem solving as well as access to specialists in curriculum and behavior. Teams that rely on the same collection of favorite instructional tricks or strategies without understanding the exact nature of a student's problem are dispensing information but not real solutions. These teams are not effective and too often become a pro forma step on the way to a special education referral or source of frustration to referring teachers.

Individual teachers who seek help with a particular student need to be invested in solving the problem, and those teachers need to believe that the solutions to the problem are within their capacity to implement. Principals can be very important in communicating to a teacher the expectation that he or she engage in serious problem solving and consultation and be committed to using the teams' recommendations.

Principals also must ensure that consultation teams are supported. Teams need sufficient time to engage in discussions with one another as well as with parents and other experts. Teams may need access to specific information or resources to help them design interventions, and they need to see that their activities are valued and yield results in terms of improved student achievement or behavior.

Special and General Coteaching

A common collaboration model is coteaching between general and special educators. As the name implies, coteaching means at least one general and one special education teacher together providing instruction to a group of special and general education students in the same classroom. The principles of coteaching are similar to team teaching with the exception that the special educator's *primary* responsibility is to ensure that students with disabilities in the classroom are accessing the general education curriculum and otherwise working toward the goals of their IEPs. The coteaching model offers opportunities to meet the needs of a diverse group of students. Research is not conclusive regarding the effectiveness of coteaching. In part, this is due to the various approaches to coteaching, as well as the "poor" implementation of the model.

Marilyn Friend has been developing and researching coteaching strategies for many years. She and Lynne Cook (1996) describe five approaches to coteaching: (1) one teaching-one supporting, (2) station teaching, (3) parallel teaching, (4) alternative teaching, and (5) team teaching.

One teaching-one supporting is the most common form of coteaching and may be the easiest to implement. In this model, one teacher has the primary role of designing and delivering instruction while the second teacher floats, helping and observing individual students. A major downside to this model is that too often it is based on having all children learn the same content in the same manner. This means that the special educator's role is to help students keep up or catch up, rather than to design individualized accommodations or differentiate instruction. In some coteaching classrooms, the special education teacher begins to function almost like an instructional assistant acting totally under the direction of the general educator. Aside from the inequities in roles that this approach to coteaching may create, it does not provide opportunities for much differentiation in instruction or for more intensive instruction. The one teaching-one supporting approach to coteaching can be an acceptable approach in some instructional situations, such as when introducing a new concept, but only if both teachers engage in designing and implementing the lesson.

In station teaching, general and special education teachers divide the content of a lesson, and each is individually responsible for planning and teaching aspects of the lesson to some part of the class. Every student in the class moves through both teacher-led groups. Each teacher teaches every student but in smaller groups. In this model, the special educator functions like another teacher in terms of his or her responsibility for the curriculum. However, this approach, if used exclusively, can fail to provide the differentiated instruction or the more intense instruction that students with disabilities require.

Parallel teaching occurs when the class is divided and each teacher delivers the same content and instruction to his or her section of the class. This type of coteaching is best for drill exercises or when the content is limited to a few key facts or knowledge so that instruction for both groups of students can be similar. Again, parallel teaching can result in a lack of differentiation or additional support needed by certain students.

Alternative teaching is probably the second most common form of special and general education coteaching. In this model, special and general educators jointly plan instruction, but the special educator focuses on reteaching or reinforcing materials taught, differentiating instruction, and making curricular accommodations and modifications for small groups of students with and without disabilities who may need extra assistance. This model can be flexible and permits any student who may need some additional help to receive some additional instruction.

In implementing alternative teaching, it is important not to stigmatize students who may be in the group receiving the different instruction. It is also essential that special and general education teachers be clear about the core and essential knowledge that is the object of the particular lesson. Both teachers need to be focused on the key curriculum goals that their group of students is expected to learn.

Team teaching is a well-known strategy in general education and requires equal planning and equal roles in implementing instruction. In fact, in a team teaching arrangement, individual teams may use all or any of the strategies discussed earlier. Teachers trade off roles and groups of students.

The Role of the Principal in Coteaching

Coteaching involves much more than assigning two teachers to a classroom, and principals play a very central role in effective implementation of coteaching. First, principals must not simply assign all students with learning and behavior problems to cotaught classes. I have seen classrooms of 30 or more students where over half of the students have IEPs and 504 accommodation plans or are low achievers who have been placed together because a special educator is in the room. This is not coteaching, and it does not provide the kinds of support and intense instruction these students need.

Another common error is to assign one special educator to coteach across several classrooms without adequate time to collaborate or plan and problem-solve with leaders. Assigning one special educator to a grade-level or subject-matter team can be very effective as long as team members plan instruction together, including how they will coteach.

Effective coteaching requires training and preparation and not just two teachers agreeing to "give it a try." Some common complaints from teachers about coteaching are as follows:

- Lack of adequate time to talk and plan
- Lack of mutual respect
- Lack of shared goals or objectives for students in the class
- Lack of conflict resolution and communication strategies
- Inequity in task distribution
- Too many difficult students in a classroom

These can be avoided with planning and administrative support.

Box 3.9   Frequently Asked Questions About Coteaching

Murawski and Dieker developed an excellent question-and-answer list for teachers and principals regarding coteaching (see http://www.dldcec.org/pdf/teaching_how-tos/murawski_36–5.pdf):

- Assess the current environment. What type of collaboration currently exists between general and special education?
- Has there been any discussion of inclusion, collaboration, or coteaching?
- How do teachers react when they hear about students with special needs in general education classes? Are there any who react favorably?
- What is our joint understanding of coteaching as a service delivery model?
- May I teach or coteach a lesson with you?
- Are there any areas that you feel less strongly about, in which I might be able to assist?
- How is the district addressing the least restrictive environment (LRE) mandate and the inclusive movement?
- Would our school site be willing to be proactive by including coteaching?
- What discipline areas will we target first?
- How will we ensure that support is provided across all content areas, including electives?
- Would we be able to count on administrative support, especially with coplanning time and scheduling assistance?
- Could we complete a coteaching checklist to help guide us in discussing our personal and professional preferences?
- Are there any pet peeves or issues that I should know prior to our working together?
- Do we both have the same level of expertise about the curriculum and instructing students with disabilities?
- How shall we ensure that we both are actively involved and neither feels overutilized or underutilized?
- What feedback structure can we create to assist in our regular communication?
- How often will coteaching occur (e.g., daily, a few times a week, for a specific unit)?

(Continued)

(Continued)

- What schedule would best meet the needs of the class and both instructors?
- How can we ensure that this schedule will be maintained consistently so that both teachers can trust it?
- How will we maintain communication between cotaught sessions?

Any or all of the aforementioned approaches will be effective only if the collaborating teachers have equal status in the classroom and recognize what knowledge and skills each brings to the collaborative effort. General and special education collaboration requires sound knowledge of the curriculum and how to assess student skills and to monitor progress, as well as a range of strategies that differentiate instruction for individual students.

There are some cautions for principals when considering collaborative approaches. First, neither schools nor individual teachers should become locked into one approach to collaboration. More important, general education teachers should not depend solely on having a special education teacher in the class to be responsible for instructing the students with disabilities. Principals must set the expectations that all teachers are responsible for all students. They should support and encourage a variety of collaborative instructional approaches. They also need to help teachers with the logistics of collaboration and provide individuals or a whole faculty with the professional development they require to build their collaborative skills.

This section has discussed three things that must be in place to have a high-quality and effective special education program: evidence-based practice, a deep understanding of how to interpret evidence, and a collaborative culture. Building leaders need to be able to judge whether their schools are implementing these practices. The principal needs to be able to judge the level of evidence supporting the instructional strategies, curriculum materials, and other resources that teachers are using. Principals also need to be able to step back from the masses of data that are increasingly available to them and ask the basic questions put forth in this section about why and how they want to use their information. Finally, principals need to recognize if special education programs, the students served by these programs, and their parents and families are left out or marginalized in their school.

Summary

The information in this book is intended to provide principals with the basic foundations of current special education practice.

In deciding what to include in this book, I was influenced by my own experience in schools and by the Educational Leadership Constituents Council standards for Advanced Programs in Educational Leadership. These standards strongly endorse the responsibility of school leaders to ensure the success of *every* student. The standards recognize that school leaders must ground their work in improving teaching and learning in their schools and must advocate for all students in their schools.

Today's principal must also promote a vision of learning that is shared and supported by the entire school community. The principal must provide the vision for effective special education and must also create and sustain an organization that respects all students, families, teachers, and staff, and fosters collective responsibility.

So, let's return to Mr. Baker and his middle school. Now that he has learned some important characteristics of special education, how might he respond to the question he had about special education students in his building?

Mr. Baker always understood that the IEPs of the students with disabilities in his school were very important documents. But he now has a better understanding that those IEPs should directly relate to the curriculum in all subjects but with a particular focus on reading, writing, and mathematics, where test scores show that these students have big deficits.

He assembles his special education teachers to review the most recent assessment data and discuss how they think the IEPs are connected to the assessment data as well as to discuss with those teachers what they perceive to be the reason for the low achievement. He also visits classrooms to see how students with disabilities are receiving instruction in reading, writing, and math. He finds a very "mixed bag" in terms of instruction. Some students with disabilities are being instructed in the core content areas by special education teachers, using a variety of commercial and teacher-made materials, including some reading materials and textbooks they have obtained from the elementary school. A group of seventh-grade special education students are enrolled in a sixth-grade general education math class cotaught by a sixth-grade math teacher and a special education teacher. A number of other special education students are in content-specific general education classrooms with paraeducators assigned to them who appear to be providing the content instruction to their students.

Mr. Baker understands that students with disabilities require individualized instructional arrangements, but he is not so sure that the different arrangements reflect what students need or whether there is any evidence that the arrangements are effective. The multiple arrangements seem to be a result of staffing and scheduling and not based on any data. Also, instruction seems loosely coupled to the curriculum and the achievement standards. Special education teachers do seem to be very proud of the amount of inclusion they have achieved in the school, but Mr. Baker wants more than inclusion. He wants to improve the achievement of students with disabilities, and he realizes that this will be a complex task involving the entire school staff. He also knows that the parents and families of the students with disabilities must be involved at every step. Mr. Baker decides that he needs more data before he can begin.

First, he administers a brief anonymous questionnaire to all of his teachers, asking them to what degree they feel responsible for the achievement of all students and for the behavior of all students. He also asks them to list the top three issues in terms of instructional concerns and the top three concerns with respect to school climate and discipline. To his surprise he finds a marked difference between his general and special educators in terms of the degree to which they perceive that all teachers are responsible for all students. Special education teachers believe that they alone are responsible for students with disabilities. They also list the following among their top three instructional issues: lack of appropriate curricular materials for students with disabilities, lack of parental cooperation and involvement, and lack of cooperation among some general education teachers. General education teachers list the following: lack of support for difficult students, lack of parental support, and homework.

Using this information, Mr. Baker brings together a group of general and special education teachers, the school's psychologist, and his assistant principal. Mr. Baker presents the following issues that he wants the team to address: the disconnect between special and general education instruction, an increase in progress monitoring, more collaboration between general and special education teachers in content instruction, and more students with disabilities receiving instruction in grade-level content. He also wants to address the issue of parental involvement. He asks the team to help him develop a set of goals to address the issues and to develop a schoolwide professional development plan and timeline to meet the goals.

Mr. Baker's vision for his middle school is one in which special education students continuously progress in general education as evidenced by improved test scores and individual student curriculum-based assessments. His vision also includes special and general education working in tandem to improve the learning outcomes of all students in his school. He articulates this vision to all staff at his next faculty meeting.

He speaks to the importance of special and general education sharing a common language about curriculum and instruction and sharing goals for improving the programs in the school and the achievement of all students. Mr. Baker asks for teachers' input regarding professional development that would include all teachers.

Throughout this journey of school improvement, Mr. Baker tells his staff that they must carefully assess progress toward all the improvement goals. Teacher attitudes, student learning and behavior, and parental perceptions of school climate must be monitored.

Mr. Baker now understands that quality special education cannot be created or sustained in isolation within a school. His commitment to effective leadership and adherence to the principles of holding high standards for every student and belief in the power of a collaborative organization means that Mr. Baker has captured the new vision for special education leadership.

Glossary

Access to the General Education Curriculum The IDEA requires that IEP teams consider how each student who receives special education will access and progress in the general education curriculum, defined as the content and instruction delivered in general education classes. Students with disabilities are to access the curriculum regardless of the setting in which they are being educated.

Accommodation A device or support that is provided to a student with a disability in instruction and during assessments that is intended to offset the impact of the disability. An accommodation is not to change the construct being measured or taught or to lower the performance standard.

Adaptation Sometimes used instead of modification, it implies that general education content or instruction has been altered in some way for one or more students. It usually means that content or performance standards have been changed.

Alternate Assessment Permitted under both IDEA and NCLB, these assessments are to be administered to students with disabilities for whom the general state or district assessments are not valid or do not reflect the curriculum of the child. These are intended for 1% or fewer of the students with disabilities.

Applied Research Research that applies or tests theory to solve real-world problems. Applied research is rigorous and employs scientific methods, but it is not primarily concerned with building new theoretical constructs.

Assistive Technology Any tool, device, or piece of equipment that can increase or improve the ability of a student with a disability to perform functions of daily living, including those involved with learning.

Availability Heuristic An error of judgment often made by decision makers attempting to judge the frequency or likelihood of an event. People making this error tend to be influenced by the availability of that event in their immediate environment, which causes them to make inaccurate judgments about incidence or cause-and-effect relationships.

Behavior Disorders Often used interchangeably with *emotional disturbance* or *emotionally handicapped,* to mean students whose primary disability is in the area of adjustment and social and behavioral skills. Some states and professionals use this term in place of emotional disturbance because they believe it to be more descriptive of the nature of the students' disabilities.

Behavior Modification   Specific procedures used to manage or eliminate unacceptable behaviors. The procedures are based on principles of behavioral psychology and involve identification of specific behaviors that are to be changed and systematic application of consequences, either positive or negative, that will reduce the behavior.

Cognitive Disability   Often used to refer to students with mild to very marked mental retardation. A cognitive disability reflects limits in performing cognitive tasks, including but not limited to areas of memory; learning new tasks; making associations between events, facts, or concepts; and drawing inferences, as well as limits in adaptive behavior or the skills required for daily living. A more current term that has been adopted is *students with intellectual disabilities.*

Collective Responsibility   A term first coined by Dr. Valerie Lee to reflect the degree to which teachers perceive that their colleagues in their school share responsibility for the achievement of all students. High collective responsibility ratings among teachers have been correlated with higher levels of achievement.

Consultation   Two or more teachers and other professional staff engaging in planning and problem-solving discussions, usually around a single child or a small group of children that is experiencing learning or behavior difficulties.

Coteaching   A model of classroom instruction in which special and general education teachers share instructional responsibilities within the same class-room. There can be several types of coteaching arrangements within a room. The key feature is that both the general and the special education teacher have equal responsibility and authority for planning and implementing instruction.

Data   The numerical results of measurements or observations. In schools, data usually refer to assessment scores; census, enrollment, or attendance rates; results of parent surveys; or a wide range of demographic indicators.

Decision Rules   Rules that are established ahead of time that guide a decision when it is needed. Decision rules often are used to assist with interpretation of data.

Early Intervening Services (EIS)   A provision added to the 2004 IDEA designed to reduce the disproportionate representation of minority students in special education. Under EIS, a school district may use up to 15% of the federal special education funds it receives each year, "to develop and implement coordinated, early intervening services, which may include interagency financing structures, for students in kindergarten through grade 12 (with a particular emphasis on students in kindergarten through grade three) who are not currently identified as needing special education or related services, but who need additional academic and behavioral support to succeed in a general education environment" (Individuals with Disabilities Education Improvement Act of 2004).

Experimental Design Research   Systematic scientific inquiry in which at least one independent variable is manipulated and other variables are held constant or controlled. The effect of this manipulation is then observed on one or more dependent variables.

Free and Appropriate Public Education (FAPE)   This is the basic legal entitlement of each child with a disability who is determined to be eligible to receive special education. The term *appropriate* is interpreted to mean that each child with a disability must have an individual education program designed by a team of individuals, including the child's special and general education teachers, other specialists as needed, and parents.

Functional Behavioral Analysis (FBA)   This approach to problem behavior is required under the IDEA for children who are known to have behavior problems, but also in conjunction with the IDEA discipline requirements. FBA requires that the IEP team look beyond the behavior that a child is exhibiting to identify specific correlates or causes of that behavior as well as conditions that seem to maintain or support the behavior. The purpose is to develop a comprehensive plan that will address the causes and consequences of problem behaviors and not simply be reactive.

Inclusion   This term can have varied meanings, although the core of inclusion is that every child with a disability is expected to be educated within a regular public school in natural proportions. That means that students with disabilities should be in their home school and not comprise more than approximately 10% of a school's population. Inclusion is also interpreted to mean that a student with a disability receives 80% or more of his or her education within the general education classroom.

Individualized Educational Program (IEP)   Each child with a disability who qualifies for special education or related services is entitled to an IEP. This is a personalized plan that directs the child's education. The IEP specifies annual goals (and objectives for students with significant cognitive disabilities who are held to "alternate achievement standards" under the NCLB) and a description of the services that will be provided to enable the student to accomplish those goals. The IEP also must include a statement of the student's present level of educational performance in the general curriculum and a description of any accommodations or modifications that may be required to enable participation in district or state assessments. The IEP is a legal document that holds the school accountable for providing educational services that are likely to enable the child to progress in the general education curriculum.

Individuals with Disabilities Education Act (IDEA)   This is the federal law that governs how special education is to be defined and implemented within individual states. In the 2004 amendments, the name was changed to the Individuals with Disabilities Education Improvement Act, so sometimes individuals refer to the law as IDEIA. The law contains the following parts: Part B provides grants to states for preschool programs and school-age programs. This part contains the basic legal entitlements for students and procedures that schools must follow. Part C provides grants to states for programs for infants and toddlers with disabilities and developmental delays. Part D contains a number of discretionary programs such as technical assistance and personnel development designed to help school districts build capacity in the area of special education.

Information   Data summaries, reports, graphs, tables, or descriptions that improve the knowledge of the people using it so they are better able to make a decision. Principals need to know which data are important and which are not useful to their school improvement efforts. Only those data that improve decision making would be considered information.

Learning Disabilities   Also referred to as specific learning disabilities, this is one of the federal categories of disability eligible to receive special education under the IDEA. Students with this disability also represent the largest proportion (over 50%) of all students who are receiving special education.

Least Restrictive Environment (LRE)   A requirement in the IDEA that, "To the maximum extent appropriate, children with disabilities, including children in public or private institutions or other care facilities, are educated with children who are not disabled, and special classes, separate schooling, or other removal of children with disabilities from the regular educational environment occurs only when the nature or severity of the disability of a child is such that education in regular classes with the use of supplementary aids and services cannot be achieved satisfactorily" (Individuals with Disabilities Education Improvement Act of 2004). The federal government measures LRE in terms of the percentage of time that students with disabilities are educated outside of general education classrooms (e.g., more than 60%, 21%–60%, 21% or less), or in separate schools, residential facilities, and home or hospitals. The IDEA regulations state that school districts make available a continuum of placements or settings.

Mainstreaming   This is another term that pertains to LRE and has traditionally been used to refer to students with disabilities moving from a special education class into a general education classroom or other setting, such as the lunchroom or recess. Mainstreaming differs from inclusion in that it assumes that a student with a disability is assigned to a special education classroom and only leaves for certain times or certain activities. Inclusion assumes that a student with a disability is assigned to a regular classroom and is a member of that class and may only leave that setting for a specific activity.

Modification   This term refers to adjustments that are made to curriculum or assessment that alters either the construct being taught and assessed or the level of performance expected.

Office of Civil Rights (OCR)   An office within the U.S. Department of Education that is charged with ensuring compliance with all civil rights laws among schools and school districts. This office has specific responsibility for monitoring school district's implementation of Section 504 of the Vocational Rehabilitation Act of 1973.

Peer Review   The process of subjecting research findings to scrutiny by a panel of experts who can judge the validity of claims made by a researcher. Peer review is considered a minimally necessary attribute of scientific validation. All reputable, scholarly journals subject articles to peer review prior to publication. Similarly, most respected scientific meetings require proposals to be peer reviewed.

Positive Behavioral Supports   Also referred to as positive behavior interventions and supports (PBIS). This is a schoolwide approach to dealing with problem behaviors that employs a three-tiered set of interventions. Primary prevention strategies are designed for an estimated 80%–90% of students in the school who behave appropriately most of the time but need some basic rules and procedures to maintain order. Secondary level strategies are designed for 5%–15% of students who are at risk of more serious behavior problems and need group-oriented specialized interventions. Tertiary strategies include individual strategies such as counseling and behavior plans and are targeted at 1%–7% of the students who have chronic and severe behavior problems.

Program Evaluation   The systematic collection and analysis of data for the purpose of making decisions about the value of a project or program. Evaluation research generally focuses on estimating the success in accomplishment of established program or project goals.

Proven Instructional Practices   Teaching and administrative practices that have been subjected to scientific testing and found to be consistently effective. Proven instructional practices produce the kinds of effects they claim, across many applications. Proven instructional practices have been validated by scientific studies and examined by the larger educational community.

Qualitative Research   Scientific investigation that relies on the collection of narratives in naturalistic settings through first-person observations. Qualitative research typically does not entail extensive analysis of numerical data. Inferences developed in qualitative research tend to rely on inductive rather than deductive reasoning.

Quantitative Research   Scientific investigation that entails collection of numerical data. Often quantitative research involves statistics and numerical analysis. Inferences derived from quantitative research are based on interpretation of data.

Random Error   Events or variables other than those of interest to the researcher or decision maker that affect an assessment or measurement outcome. Random error is present in all data systems, and the decision maker never knows for sure how much random error is present. Therefore, all assessment systems must include procedures to control for random error. Systems that are highly reliable are said to contain little random error.

Related Services   Defined under the IDEA as services that are provided free of charge and include transportation and such developmental, corrective, and other supportive services as may be required to assist a child with a disability to benefit from special education. Related services include various therapies, recreation and therapeutic recreation, social work and counseling services, and medical services that may be required for diagnoses or evaluation of a disability.

Reliability   The minimally essential ingredient for determining data quality. Reliability is an index of the amount of random error that an assessment system contains. Often, reliability is interpreted as relating to the stability or consistency of a test or assessment procedure. A test is reliable if it yields the same kind of results time after time.

Replication   The process of repeating studies using similar methods but different participants. Similar findings found in multiple replications are thought to be more scientifically valid than results that have been reported in only one or a few studies.

Representative Sample   A subset of the larger group about whom a researcher is interested that shares all the critical characteristics of that larger group. A sample is considered representative when observations about it can be applied validly to the larger population from which it is drawn.

Representativeness Heuristic   The mistake people commit when they make a decision on the basis of superficial or extraneous characteristics that seem to make a particular example *a representative* of the larger category.

Response to Intervention (RtI)   A method for determining eligibility for special education, specifically for students suspected of having a learning disability, sometimes called Response to Instruction. The central purpose of RtI is to rule out the referrals to special education of students who are not learning due to poor or inadequate instruction. RtI focuses on how a student responds to systematic and increasingly more intensive levels of instructional interventions that are implemented by general education teachers. The interventions are usually referred to as "tiers" and typically there are three tiers of increasingly intensive instruction.

Scientific Validation   The process of verifying the truthfulness of a theory or practice through systematic research methods. Typically, scientific validation entails publication of results in peer reviewed publications or presentation of results at scientific meetings.

Section 504   Refers to Section 504 of the Vocational Rehabilitation Act of 1973, which states that, "No qualified handicapped person shall, on the basis of handicap, be excluded from participation in, be denied the benefits of, or otherwise be subjected to discrimination under any program or activity which receives Federal financial assistance." Students with disabilities are covered under Section 504 whether or not they are found to be eligible for special education. Section 504 entitles a student to an individual accommodation plan, which is to determine what accommodations are required in instruction, setting or facilities, and assessments. Section 504 also protects the rights of adults with disabilities.

Special Education   Specially designed instruction, at no cost to parents, to meet the unique needs of a child with a disability.

Students With Disabilities   There are 13 federally defined categories of disabilities under IDEA: mental retardation, hearing impairments (including deafness), speech or language impairments, visual impairments (including blindness), emotional disturbance, orthopedic impairments, autism, traumatic brain injury, other health impairments, specific learning disabilities, multiple disabilities, deaf-blindness, and developmental delay.

Universal Design   Designed-in flexibility to accommodate the instructional needs of many diverse learners in a single product or approach. Products and environments are designed to be usable by the largest number of people possible without the need for additional modifications beyond those incorporated into the original design. When additional adaptations are needed, they can be easily and unobtrusively accommodated by the original design.

Validity   The quality of a decision or inference that lends it credence, validity is roughly analogous to truthfulness. While validity often is treated as an attribute inherent to tests, it is more accurate to refer to the validity of decisions based on some data or information. Validity involves both empirical data and logical reasoning, No matter how well intentioned, decisions that are based on bad data cannot be valid. For example, a well-designed assessment could be used to make poor decisions.

References

Americans with Disabilities Act of 1990, 42 U.S.C. § 12101 *et seq.* (1990).

Board of Education of the Hendrick Hudson School District v. Rowley, 458 U.S. 176 (1982).

Brookhart v. Illinois State Board of Education, 697 F.2d 179 (7th Cir. 1983).

Chapman et al. v. California Department of Education (No. C 01–01780 CRB, N.D. California, February 21, 2002).

Council of Administrators of Special Education (CASE). (2006a). *Promoting student access: A resource guide for educators (Section 504 and Americans with Disabilities Act)*. Fort Valley, GA: Author.

Council of Administrators of Special Education (CASE). (2006b). *Response to intervention: Policy considerations and implementation.* Fort Valley, GA: Author.

Debra P. v. Turlington, 654 F.2d 1079 (5th Cir. 1981).

Education for All Handicapped Children Act, 20 U.S.C. § 1401 *et seq.* (1975).

Friend, M., & Cook, L. (1996). *Interactions: Collaboration skills for school professionals* (2nd ed.). White Plains, NY: Longman.

Fuchs, D., & Deshler, D. D. (2007). What we need to know about responsiveness to intervention (and shouldn't be afraid to ask). *Learning Disabilities Research & Practice, 22*(2), 129–136.

Honig v. Doe, 479 U.S. 1084 (1988).

Hocutt, A. M. (1996). Effectiveness of special education: Is placement the critical factor? *Special Education for Students with Disabilities, 6*(1), 77–102.

Huefner, D. S. (2005). *Getting comfortable with special education law: A framework for working with children with disabilities* (2nd. Ed.) Norwood, MA: Christopher-Gordon Publishers, Inc.

Husen, T., & Postlethwaite, T. N. (Eds.). (1994). *International encyclopedia of education* (2nd ed.). Oxford, UK: Pergamon.

Hunt, E. S. (1996). *A guide to the international interpretation of U.S. education program data: CIP, IPEDS, CCD, and ISCED.* Washington, DC: U.S. Department of Education, Office of Educational Research and Improvement, Center for National Education Statistics, Office of Research.

Individualized Education Program (IEP), U.S. Department of Education, Office of Special Education Programs, Retrieved May 14, 2008, http://idea.ed.gov/explore/view/p/%2Croot%2Cdynamic%2CTopicalBrief%2C10%2C

Individuals with Disabilities Education Act, 1400 34 C.F.R. Part 300 (1997).

Individuals with Disabilities Education Act Amendments of 1997, 20 U.S.C. § 1401(a)(17) (1998).

Individuals with Disabilities Education Improvement Act of 2004, 20 U.S.C. § 1400 (2004).

Lee, V. E., & Loeb, S. (2000). School size in Chicago elementary schools effects on teachers' attitudes and students' achievement. *American Educational Research Journal, 37,* 5–31.

Nader, R. (1965). *Unsafe at any speed.* New York: Grossman.

Nelson, J. R., Martella, R. M., & Marchand-Martella, N. (2002). Maximizing student learning: The effects of a comprehensive school-based program for preventing problem behaviors. *Journal of Emotional and Behavioral Disorders, 10*(3), 136–148.

Nolet, V., & McLaughlin, M. J. (2005). *Accessing the general curriculum: Including students with disabilities in standards-based reform* (2nd ed.). Thousand Oaks, CA: Corwin Press.

Rene v. Reed, 751 N.E. 2d 736 (Ind. App. June 20, 2001).

Tufte, E. R. (1997). *Visual and statistical thinking: Displays of evidence for making decisions.* Cheshire, CT: Graphics Press.

Tufte, E. R. (2001). *The visual display of quantitative information* (2nd ed.). Cheshire, CT: Graphics Press.

U.S. Department of Education. (2004). *Building the legacy: IDEA 2004. Part B: Identification of specific learning disabilities.* Retrieved February 12, 2008, from http://idea.ed.gov/explore/view/p/,root,dynamic,TopicalBrief,23

U.S. Department of Education. (2005). *US Department of Education's fiscal year 2005 performance and accountability report.* Washington, DC: Author.

Vocational Rehabilitation Act of 1973, Section 504, 29 U.S.C. § 794(a) (1996).

Yell, M. (2006). *The law and special education* (2nd ed.). Upper Saddle River, NJ: Pearson Education, Inc.

Index